T0165463

# BRONX MAN

by
Marty Toohey

Order this book online at www.trafford.com
or email orders@trafford.com

Most Trafford titles are also available at major online book retailers.

Printed in the United States of America.

ISBN: 978-1-4269-8877-6 (sc)
ISBN: 978-1-4269-8879-0 (e)

Library of Congress Control Number: 2011913725

*Trafford rev. 08/11/2011*

 www.trafford.com

**North America & international**
toll-free: 1 888 232 4444 (USA & Canada)
phone: 250 383 6864 ♦ fax: 812 355 4082

# Contents

# INTRODUCTION

A father and his five kids plan a strategy

The writing part is over. Now comes the hard Part – the title and the introduction.

How can I write an introduction to a book that has fifty unrelated chapters? Short Stories is a nice title but it's common. I am not a commoner. I thought of having my name occupy the entire front cover in a blazing metallic orange. Everyone would see it and I need all the help I can get.

I sent a copy of every chapter, as I wrote it, to my daughter Chris for her critique. She was ruthless; just what I needed: confusing, so-so, gibberish, Bingo! wrong substitute, doesn't flow, deadly. She graded me a C- on most. But I got one Bingo! That was encouraging.

If you don't like my book imagine how it would read without Chris' input.

I became addicted to this book. I loved writing it; hated my computer's participation. I did spend too much time writing it. I left dishes in the sink, sox and shorts everywhere. The kitchen needed help. My son Terrence came by. He looked around and said, "Give it a rest! You're living like Edgar Allen Poe and you're not even famous." He saw a collection of unread newspapers still in my mailbox.

"YF, have your cleaning girl come over." (She was here yesterday but I didn't wanna tell him.)

I tried writing a chapter on being in the Navy. "You sound like a sea cadet," they said. "Write about being a kid in the Bronx," suggested Anne Marie, I told her that's what my first book was about. If you read it you'd know!

"Don't they publish re-runs in books the way they do in TV?" asked Terrence.

I always wanted to be a foreign correspondent, I told them I wrote three chapters on current wars: Afghanistan, Sri Lanka, Iraq. My son Tim entered the room as I mentioned war.

"What's war got to do with your book?" he asked.

"I wrote chapters on golf and jazz and my book's not on either one.

"What are you calling it?" Anne Marie asked. He doesn't know, someone said. "I guess it's a mystery," Anne Marie said.

Terrence asked, "Chris, do you get credit if the book is a best-seller?" Anne Marie wanted to know who gets the blame if the book is a dud?

"Suppose it wins he Pulitzer Prize," asked Chris. "I think it can win the Pulitzer. The Nobel Prize for major accomplishments like discoveries in medicine," said Terrence. "I think anybody can win the Pulitzer," he added.

"Too bad Patty isn't here, YF. She'd want you to make it a business book. Business is a hobby with her."

Someone asked if the Gallery Restaurant would display the book. I said they probably would. "How do you split he money if they sell some books." I thought 50-50 and said so. "I think you should get 75-25," said Terrence. "You wrote the book."

Somebody asked how much the Pulitzer Prize is worth. " Maybe $50,000, or $100,000. Whatever.

"Gee, an hour ago I was perfectly willing to break even. You kids helped me see my potential. Where do you think I should hang my Pulitzer Prize?"

# FUELING AT SEA

Our prime job during a sea detail in 1946 was to fuel the F.D.R. at speed while both ships were underway. F.D.R was the largest aircraft carrier in the fleet. It earned its stripes in the Pacific during the closing months of World War II.

FDR's fighter pilots had outstanding   reputations for attacking and sinking Japanese ships during battles.  As the fleet approached more than a dozen or more fighting ships appeared on the horizon. I was standing watch on the port side of our ship's bridge. Through my binoculars I saw what could be described as a threatening sight. I wondered how the enemy felt, only one year ago during wartime, at this horrific threat about to attack.

But this was only a sea detail. Two destroyers, known as "tin cans", sat far in the rear of the fleet. Without warning, each destroyer cut a high-speed swath through the Mediterranean and landed in front of the carrier each assuming a guardian position in a few seconds.

The sea was rough which made it more difficult for both the Pawcatuck and the FDR to maintain identical speeds and bearings, mandatory for fueling at sea.

The F.D.R. resembled a massive city as it approached the Pawcatuck. Specifications of both ships later told the tale. The carrier had a displacement of 45,000 tons and was 968 feet long. The Pawcatuck was almost half its size, measuring 553 feet in length and displacing only 7,256 tons. As the carrier continued to move closer to us, sailors on the bridge joked that one could place our ship on the flight deck of the F.D.R. and still have room to launch a squadron of fighter planes.

Once both ships were cruising at identical speeds, as if in a photo finish, both Captains agreed on the speed and course direction we were cruising. This critical point of information was relayed to each helmsman and fed into the Pawcatuck's master automatic gyrocompass that was kept in a steel enclosure for safety purposes. Our Captain, a salty old sailor named McKinney, asked that a first class boatswain mate take the wheel. A less experienced seaman was relieved in light of the seriousness of the sea detail.

Gunner First Class Hopkins prepared to fire the steel rod across the water onto the bridge of the F.D.R. Unfortunately, the steel rod, from the shot, hit a bulkhead just several feet from the target and bounced off the carrier into the Mediterranean— a bad omen if one believes in such things. Gunner Hopkins reeled the rod back on board and prepared to fire another shot from his air rifle. This time he hit the target and the fueling exercise was officially underway. I relayed to the Officer of the Deck the progress being made on deck. Our ship's deck apes guided the hose to our tank and coupled.

Winches on board the aircraft carrier began to pull the fuel line over the sea, first the small hemp line and then the first length of thick, heavy eight-inch rubber hose, interior lined with steel mesh.

Steel couplings were guided on board after being connected to the carrier. The moment the connection was made, both ships cruised as one. Should the helmsman on either ship so much as cruise a single degree off course a catastrophic accident would occur. Once the fuel lines were connected, the deck hands on the Pawcatuck turned on the fuel line, as though turning on a giant faucet, and oil began flowing to the F.D.R., slowly at first, but soon gushing from the fuel tanks on board our ship to the empty tanks of the carrier.

All went well during the first twenty minutes. Each helmsman kept their ship precisely on course. The automatic gyrocompass guided the Pawcatuck's course direction. Sailors on both ships, who were not otherwise occupied, lined the rails to watch the exercise.

Both Captains agreed that communications between the ships' sea detail was going very well. Our Captain had me contact the lower deck to proceed with caution. The hose line would eventually be directed to an oil tank on our lower deck I heard the Captain's response through my headset and was pleased. Then, out of the blue came an explosive sound of screaming metal on metal. It was quickly discerned, by the helm, that the gyrocompass had failed inside its steel enclosure. Now the helmsman was on his own and tried to keep the ship on course relying only on the ship's magnetic compass. Ever mindful that a degree or two, one way or the other, could end in disaster the helmsman's eyes were glued to the compass points. Sure enough, the Pawcatuck began to drift ever so slightly to starboard. The Captain ordered the helmsman to try to get back on course. It took two men to turn the wheel and get the ship back on course only to be shoved by the sea in the opposite direction.

Now the ship was sliding to port toward the F.D.R.'s stern on a collision course. The rough seas pushed both ships in two directions making it impossible to maintain course. The Pawcatuck drifted too far back to starboard, away from the F.D.R. The fuel line pulled tight then stretched to a rigid state over the ocean. It stretched tightly across the water like a high wire before it finally snapped. The coupling on the F.D.R. that connected the hose line had required a small crane to lift it for installation. The coupling was ripped from its housing and tossed backwards toward the Pawcatuck like a child's play toy.

A ten-inch hose lined on the inside with steel mesh and on the outside with inch-thick industrial rubber flew into the air. It resembled an animal trainer's whip that snapped and crackled, crashing down on our lower deck as a geyser of oil from the fuel inside escaped  The oil poured skyward like it had been shot from a twelve-inch cannon flooded the main deck.

The hose line swung back on board in fierce fashion clearing everything in its way. Steel Side rails were decapitated as the sea detail crew ran for cover. Fortunately, with the exception of slight abrasions that were quickly treated, no one was seriously injured.

Our first fueling at sea exercise had failed, a black mark on the record of the Pawcatuck, and while fueling the star of the fleet no less. Bits and pieces of what remained were pulled aboard including the elusive fuel line now in tatters from ripping through obstacles in its path.

With no fuel line to resume the sea detail, no gyrocompass to insure accuracy, the Pawcatuck was ordered to hobble back to a local port for repair. Just another auxiliary oiler, a working ship among the more romantic vessels that have an entire city of spectators turn out to see it arrive in port. Such is life aboard a working ship. But the Pawcatuck did hold hands with the glamour puss of the Pacific, if only for a few minutes.

# HITCHHIKER

Traffic was light. Arnie raised his arm and stuck out his thumb. The first three cars passed him as if he was a corner mailbox. He wore his Navy uniform to gain attention but so did everyone else in this Navy town.

An Eldorado arrived at speed, slammed on the brakes and screeched to an instant halt.

"Hey, Podner, hop in!" The driver wore a cowboy hat that appeared to be six sizes too large. He slumped behind the wheel and tried to act cool as if he was posing for a Marlboro ad.

Arnie laughed at him. "Forget your horse, cowboy?" He'd have thrown him a pack of Marlboros but he quit smokin' a few years ago. They claim the second-hand smoke in bars sticks to your lungs until you're about thirty, and then you die.

He remained slumped way down in his seat as though he had osteoporosis. His hat covered his eyes the way Clint Eastward might wear it if he played a retarded cowboy. The Hat invited Arnie to jump into the Eldo. He did.

He tossed his peacoat on the empty seat and no sooner sat down when the driver crushed the accelerator with the heel of his long leather boot. The Eldo went from nothing to 90 mph in a heartbeat. Arnie watched the speedometer climb to 105. It felt like the car was going to lift off.

"We're going to the moon, buddy boy. At least you are!"

Arnie planned to meet his shipmates at a beer joint called the Laredo Bar, about fifteen minutes away. At this speed he thought they could overshoot the Caribbean Sea and wind up in Brazil.

"Don't get any smart-ass ideas, buddy boy," said the Hat.

"There's a spigot on the floorboard aimed at your pretty boy face. I can turn the juice on in a flash with my left pinky. Carbolic acid will spray onto your face. They tell me it eels like water, at first. Then it burns the skin off your face off in seconds. You can hear it sizzle. So don't get any ideas, buddy boy."

Arnie didn't utter a word. He was numb with fear. What in the hell just happened, he wondered? The hat's jacket featured scrambled gold braids on the sleeves. He looked like a doorman at the Copacabana. His leather boots had huge high heels and appeared too big. Arnie figured he must have robbed a size 48 mannequin for his 36-short body.

"I'll try to help you best I can," said the Hat. " You look like a nice kid. Navy boy, too," he said. "I can tell you this. If you jump out the door at speed, you won't have a bone in your body that's not broken in two or three places," he said. "If you live, re-hab could take forever." Arnie tried to think about it but instead thought about his wife and wondered if he had a Will.

"Fall out the wrong way like my last guy did and you'll look like someone sewed your ass to your face!" So Arnie wasn't the Hat's first victim. He felt his cheeks curl around his nose, and his ears fold over his eyes. He almost got sick.

It sounded as if the Hat forced his victims out the side door.

"The second best way to get out is to jump feet first," said the Hat. "You might save your face that way," he continued, "but no guarantees." Arnie thought of climbing quickly into the back of the Eldo and grabbing the Hat from behind. But how does he stop the car? He thought of throttling the mad man and hoping for the best. But the speedometer still hovered between 95 and 100 mph.

"Gotta admit, pretty boy, at least I'm giving you a choice!" With that he laughed like a banshee and started rocking the car from left to right singing some kind of idiot song.

" Both ways have their advantages," he said. "But let's not quibble over proven statistics. Jumping out the side door feet first is your best bet. I've calculated this a thousand times on my computer." Arnie concluded that the Hat had to be the craziest mad man he had ever even read about. This guy sits up all night getting his kicks doing homework.

"Listen to me, buddy boy. I want what's best for you."

"Cowboy," Arnie said, "I don't find either of your two choices very appealing. Nor would my wife, the mother of our new born baby." Arnie thought he'd try a 'do it for the family' approach on the Hat.

"If you push me through the side door you'll be killing, not just one, but three people, really. Think about that," said Arnie. The Hat actually seemed to think for the first time. But he kept his fingers on the acid switch "How you figure that?" he asked.

" The judge will throw the book at you for killing me, a military man in time of war; for making my son an orphan; and making my wife a widow." Arnie let his words sink in, if that was possible. "You'll get life in prison if they don't fry your ass in the Chair -- those are your choices, cowboy." Arnie gave the Hat some time to think, if that was possible.

"Will they let me wear my hat?" asked the Hat.

"Arnie almost broke up laughing. Even when you take a shower," said Arnie.

He slowed the car down. Arnie hoped the Brazil trip was cancelled. The Hat turned and spoke.

"So ya think I'll go to prison, eh? Suppose I don't kill you? Then what?"

"Oh, you'll probably be found for reckless driving maybe, and going through a red light or two. Little bitty stuff. Get a good lawyer. You'll be out in no time. I'll put in a good word for you." The Hat relaxed his grip on the acid switch. Arnie didn't know whether to jump for his life or continue to humor this nut.

"You'll put in a good word for me? After me scaring the beeejeezus out of you? By God, you're a good friend."

Arnie thought he'd choke on that last line. He went from hopeless victim to being a buddy, inside of a minute. But the Hat was still holding him at bay. Arnie didn't think he could displace the Hat, take the wheel without winding up in a crash.

"Ya know, cowboy. If you make a plea they'll go easy on you."

"They will? Like what?"

"Well, maybe drop one or two of the charges. You could probably get out in a week."

"In a week?"

"Beats going to the chair." They were now in the downtown section of Beaumont. Police cars circled. One pulled directly in front, blocking their path. The car stopped. Arnie jumped out.

"Officer, this is the mad man you're looking for. I'm the hostage. Better search him before you stick him in the back. I'll ride up front. Check his hat. He could have an arsenal up there."

They drove to the station house. Arnie filled in the details to the satisfaction of the police who checked his record. "Wow. This guy has as many infractions as Latry King has marriages." said the policeman. "I'm glad you see it as a 'throw-away-the-key' case," said Arnie.

""Incidentally, he asked if he could wear his hat in jail."

"Are you kidding,?" replied the cop. "I said it would be OK if he kept his finger off the trigger." They all laughed.

# MARKSIE

The Japanese torpedoed the U.S.S. Orleans during the Battle of Midway in early 1942. Marksie, a Chief Petty Officer at the time, led his men over the side as soon as the public address system blared, Abandon Ship!

All four of the destroyer's lifeboats were released by boatswain mates and dropped into the water. The lifeboat Marksie expected to board was let loose in eleven seconds. Marksie smiled with satisfaction -- it was two seconds faster than earlier practice times.

Had the crew known that Marksie checked their time even under such stressful conditions, they would have kidded their taskmaster unmercifully. "We're sinking, and the Chief still insists we go down in regulation time!"

Marksie's shipmates boarded their lifeboat then plucked their Chief out of the Pacific. The survivors searched the sea for missing mates. Chief asked his rescuers to row over to where he thought he saw his buddy fly off the stern after the first explosion.

They found the young man frightened, but intact, delighted to see the rescue party. Other bodies floating near him but were lifeless. The grateful youngster scampered aboard the lifeboat with little help. Happy to be alive, the smile on his baby face was almost as wide as the lifeboat.

One of the men in the lifeboat noted the young man's buoyancy. "He probably feels he could walk on water after what he's been through!"

The kid was still panting as he asked Marksie for a cigarette. "No more cigarettes until we get rescued. Unless you like smokin' wet ones," said Marksie. The conversation soon turned to survival.

A veteran Chief Petty Officer, who was much older than Marksie, summed up some of the possibilities. ""We can sit here and hope the Nipponese aren't interested in taking us captive. That would be most unpleasant."

One of the sailors asked the Chief if he had ever been captured. The CPO unbuttoned the front of his shirt and exposed dozens of tiny scars covering his chest from his neck to his navel. His nipples had been erased. "Cigarette burns," he explained. "I wish the Japs'cigarettes were as wet as yours!" He smiled. A few on the raft forced a smile but most stared at his scars. The Chief forecasted the survival possibilities.

"The Japs could come back for target practice and pop us one by one, like fish in a barrel. They do that. So don't stop praying."

The Japanese didn't come near them. Nine seamen could not be found. This depleted the ship's crew of sixty. A dozen or so survivors sat in each boat for two days before being rescued.

Marksie had a captive audience. He re-called his dog-eared war stories. His introductions were like drinking a glass of bland water. He often forgot the punch line, but no matter to him. He laughed louder than anyone, often all by himself. A British trawler picked up their boat two days later just as Marksie ran out of jokes,

Marksie couldn't sit still. The moment the ship left the dock, he'd grow restless until he landed in a foreign port. It never mattered which port -- Marksie could find trouble anywhere in the world. In Spain he would admire a lovely dama, regardless of who her escort might be. After some vino, he'd invite the dama to a fiesta nearby even though her boyfriend, or husband, frowned on the idea.

He was a good looking guy but more important, he was still a CPO, which meant he could wear his lightly starched white dress shirt, a real tie, lines of his colorful battle ribbons and shiny brass buttons on his jacket.

Marksie's antics often stirred up a small riot and he'd have to be escorted back to the ship by the Shore Patrol. The infraction would sometimes nullify his liberty depending on the story he'd fabricate.

If he didn't find trouble in Spain, he'd use the same approach in Paris. He haunted the Parisian bistros always asking the wrong femme to danse, sil vous plait? Frenchmen, like most men, are disagreeable about parting with their femmes whether or not the intruder asked sil vous plait? More trouble.

Giving this devil his due, Marksie certainly didn't strike out all the time. He carried a .750 batting average with the ladies, according to the bean counters who checked him regularly. He felt this put him in the major leagues of lovers and he acted accordingly.

There were times when the Chief forgot that he had a ship to return to the next morning. Rumor had it that his ships left several times without him. Facts are hard to come by. There were more detentions, and in some cases, serious demotions. He eventually allowed himself to be reduced to a lowly seaman assigned to laborious jobs in the bowels of our ship.

Marksie was exceptional. He ascended five full ratings from lowly seaman painting decks to Chief Petty Officer. The crew held the CPO rating above the highest rank. CPO's were nautical guys who knew every twist and turn of life at sea. They could tie whichever knot was called for. They knew the Rules of the Road as well as they did the Los Angeles freeway or when to leave to meet her by the time she gets to Phoenix.

After a few drinks, Marksie would pontificate, which if you were in the mood, was another form of entertainment.

"Gentlemen, swagger once you ascend the lofty heights of this man's Navy. But mind ye,'tis a slippery slope once you arrive!"

Anyone attracted to Marksie's jokes and story telling always waited for him to recite his mantra before leaving.

# "Taxi Driver"

My father owned three taxicabs when he married my mother in 1927. He had to sell his taxi business when the market crashed in 1929. He never drove another cab -- never drove another car for the rest of his life. We never flound out why. But his taxi driving stories lived on until the day he died.

The last time I heard my father tell a story about picking up a fare just south of 96th Street under the 'El' on Third Avenue, was at least fifty years after it actually happened. His recall was remarkable. Details of his stories made it seem like it happened only yesterday. Listeners were given precise street locations to fit each story. It happened on the corner of Ninth Street and Leonard Place, where the old Wanamakers Department Store used to be. There was always the same policeman directing traffic off Ninth Street. He'd give me the high sign and I'd park wherever I wanted.

It was about t hree o'clock in the morning, my normal quittin' time. It was rainin' cats and dogs. I was through for the night. I had about seven blocks to drive with no visibility.

The windshield wipers couldn't manage the torrential downpour. I must have driven into some deep curbside water. It slowed the cab and sent what looked like Rockaway ocean flat up against my windshield. When it hit, it sounded like a ton of steel meeting a cement wall at forty miles an hour.

Thought I saw a vague outliine of a body about twenty or thirty feet directly in the path of my cab. He wore a look of horrror on his face waving his arms in a kind of c riss-cross pattern like a Naval signalman. I tturned the wheel hard-left, away from the guy, slammed on my brakes, which sent a screaming pitch into the air as if every cat on the east side was enjoying a bachhaal.

He stood loking at me as I barely missed him. He grabbed hold of my front fender, worked himself towatrd the back, anddamned if he didn't open the door and flop in. He was built ike a brick building. There I am, sitting four blocks from my garage on Sixty-First street, and this guy tumbles in.

"Harlem!" he mumbles. No way I'm going to Harlem at that hour but the guy's sittin' in the back of my cab."

"Just as an ambulance sped by. I decided to follow it, and I did. We both landed together outside St. Vincent's Hospital. Two attendnants came running toward the ambutlance. I called to them to come over and help me.

"Hey, this guy is part of the ambulance party. He's just too drunk to enjoy it." When they laid him on the gurney, I raced out and took off toward my garage. I thought a out it on the way home.

"If I only had the s.o.b. on the meter, I coulda made a buck."

# TAXI STORIES

Whenever my father took a break in his storytelling he maintained command of his listening audience while he tapped away the long ash on the end of his smoldering cigare.

As a kid, I'd watch his cigarette ash grow longer and longer but not break off until he finally flicked it into an ashtray. Listeners at socials were fascinated by my father's "hack stories", stories of his taxi driving days.

I picked up the President of the Harriman National Bank at the intersection of Church and Trinity, across the street from the Stock Exchange, he'd begin. That's just south of Wall Street. I often wondered whether he was telling the story to tell the story or to simply roll words like Harriman National Bank off his tongue. He punctuated his stories with a melodic cadence, laced with the speech inflections of a Bronxite. Some of the words he used had a special ring to them—Clason Point, was a neighborhood in the Bronx, Wanamakers,a popular department store where the wealthy shopped.

Wanamakers' posted a Help Wanted sign in their front window. It read Catholics Need Not Apply. That's why we didn't shop there. Couldn't afford it anyway.

Names of certain people also fit better than others. Big Wop DeCurtain was one of them. That name had to be owned by a giant of a man. It received countless mentions in stories about street fights that were always won by the big man.

So this guy pins little Johnny Isaacs to the wall for no reason at all. He was about to pulverize him when along comes Big Wop DeCurtain. Big Wop wades in and takes one look at this s.o.b., grabs him around the collar and the belt and pitches him out into the gutter. The s.o.b. takes off down Washington Avenue. We never saw him in our neighborhood again.

elebrities stepped in and out of my father's cabs, and he had a story for each one. I'll never forget the Sunday afternoon I had Jimmy Durante in my cab. I picked him up at the Astor Hotel at Forty-Fourth and Broadway. He asked me to take him to Holy Cross Church on the north side of 34th Street between Eighth and Ninth Avenue. That's only a few blocks away but I guess he didn't want to walk.

He told me his niece was getting married. The ride only took a couple of minutes and the meter read just fifty cents but Jimmy gave me a twenty-dollar bill. Told me to keep the change. Helluva nice guy.

Anyone who tipped well was a "helluva nice guy". Others were, "cheap skates" and worse. "The more they have, the less they tip," he'd say. Major league baseball players are the cheapest tippers on the face of the earth. All except the Babe, he'd quickly add. "The Babe would take out a fistful of dollar bills, ask how much he owed, and peel off a big tip no matter what the meter read.

Marty Dunn was hacking out of our garage when he picked up a fare after the Yankee game broke. It was Lou Gehrig, the Yankee first baseman, and the Yanks had just won the 1927 World Series. Marty started counting the size of his tip the minute Gehrig got into his cab.

Gehrig tells Marty to take him downtown to the Waldorf-Astoria on the east side of Park and Fifty-First street. Now that's a nice fare to have. Always good for a coupla bucks on the meter and maybe a dollar tip, depending. Marty pulls up to the Waldorf, Gehrig reads the meter, gives him two and a half bucks, the exact amount on the meter, and walks into the hotel without leaving a tip. Marty couldn't believe his eyes. So much for major league baseball players.

My father told stories about Al Jolson and Ruby Keeler, stars of the 1920's, and there were times when it wasn't clear whether he was telling a story he experienced first hand or read about it like everyone else in a Broadway gossip column.

Sophie Tucker hailed me one night outside her hotel. She was starring in a show called "Honky Tonk" at the Winter Garden. Told me she was late for her opening act. Asked me to step on it and I did. She talked all the way to the theater. She had that whiskey voice and barrel house laugh. She was a good skate. Tipped me ten dollars for helping her make the show on time. She said, "Marty, if you ever wanna drive for me, just call my manager. I could use a chauffeur like you.' I didn't take her up on it, but she did call me by name."

Taxicab owners had to buy what is still called a "medallion"—a license that gives the owner the right to operate his taxicab in New York City. The cost in my father's day must have been affordable since he owned three cabs. I'm told that today's cost is hundreds of thousand dollars.

Words like medallion and hack and hail and pickup and drop and meter and all of the street names and locations in Manhattan were part of my father's lexicon for most of his life.

I remember when I was real small, standing eye level to his weathered, tweed, taxi cap sitting on the end table in the living room after he returned each night after driving all day. A combination of scents from the worn leather, the smell of cigarettes, and the sweatband inside the cap created an aroma that was comforting and reassuring to a little boy. Forty years later I wrote a column about that cap in the magazine I worked for at the time. My father showed it to all the retired men in the neighborhood. He was surprised that I remembered his cap.

His "hack license" sat next to his cap. Photos on hack licenses were similar to photos on passports and my father's was no different. I remember looking at it and wondering why my father looked so frightened. Hack licenses fitted into a small frame near the glove compartment of the cab.

His name was printed in large black block letters—Martin M. Toohey. My middle initial is "T". It was supposed to be "M" for Michael and that would have made me Martin M. Toohey, Jr. but that's another story. A large serial number appeared on the hack license so that passengers could see it from the back seat and report drivers for rules infractions.

After driving someone else's taxicabs for a number of years, he formed a partnership with friend Marty Dunn. They bought a shooting gallery that was located in a Bronx amusement park called Starlight Park. The business failed. My father went to work for the City of New York. I never saw him at the wheel of another car after his taxi driving days. Our family never owned a car, strange for someone who once made his living driving cars. Anyone listening to my father recall his taxi driving days would assume that his present car was parked downstairs at curbside. But it never was.

# Insurance Policy

The Rock of Gibraltar never looked as imposing in real life as it did on the cover of my father's Prudential Life Insurance Policy. The document featured a four-inch silver metallic likeness of the famous Rock fastened to the cover of the policy. "I was told by Kevin Clancy, who should know since he was born over there, that it suggested a value of more than One Hundred British Pounds, Sterling," said the owner, who never hesitated to brag if it lent credence to his story.

Actually, the policy would be worth a maximum of one hundred dollars – after a lifetime of twenty-five cent installments paid to Mr. Schwartz, our Prudential Agent. He'd ring our doorbell every Saturday morning to collect a twenty-five cent installment that my mother never failed to pay on time.

My father displayed the policy before visitors every chance he got. Whenever we had guests, he'd always ask, sometimes before they got their coats off, if they cared to see The Rock of Gibraltar. Of course, the regulars to our home always agreed. There were also those who had not experienced one of his unveilings who were eager to partake in his ceremony. They soon learned it was a sacred part of their visit much as one genuflects upon entering a church.

While my mother saw to it that our guests were properly seated and served a beverage and sweets, he'd walk sprightly through our foyer, down the hall to the large bedroom. He'd open wide double doors, reach inside to an area at the back of the top shelf, retrieve a faded Miles Shoe box wrapped with two thick rubber bands, and finally carried it out into the dining room for the guests to see. This undertaking often required more than several minutes as our guests waited patiently, including those who had experienced the ordeal several times before.

Finally, my father opened the Miles Shoes box after removing particles of dust that had collected since the last showing. "Official Papers" were first extracted – birth certificates, Baptismal certificates, a marriage certificate, and social security documents. Expired rental agreements always brought a question from a grandchild who asked why Grandpa kept previous rental certificates from apartments of years gone by. He'd always answer in the same way, "Because you never know."

My father always began with a brief introduction to his topic, the way a college professor might. Once he felt he had control of his audience, the history of The Rock was discussed. He'd outline his story as though he had just returned for those who were unfamiliar.

"The Brits were ready for invasion by land or sea, or both, and God help the Germans if they chose to invade by way of the Gibraltar Strait. They'd face a wall of artillery positioned for that very purpose that could blow a German battleship into shards of steel!"

Whenever my ship passed the Rock as we left the Mediterranean Sea, having fueled in Bahrain, Arabia; or, upon entering the Strait on our way to Tangier, when we sailed by the Rock, I thought of my Dad.

My mother was not as understanding. One morning as she was about to go shopping, she noticed my father making additional notes inside the cover of the policy.

"Did you take that policy out again?" my mother asked. "You just had it out the other night. The value doesn't change. We don't get interest on it. So why bother?" He always ignored her jibes.

"I'd understand your obsession with the policy if we could put a hot dog stand on the burial site and make some money. It would give you something to do."

My mother didn't understand his desire to re-live the highlights of his years. My father reviewed chapters in his life but had to fabricate the rest from books or newspapers, to suit his fancy. On occasion he'd relate fresh true stories as told to him by a sailor son, who made it all sound exciting.

# HEADSTONE

My mother called the family together after my father had passed. His headstone had just been installed at St. Raymond's Cemetery in the Bronx.

Mom had insisted on designing the face of the headstone. She worked with the cemetery's stonecutter and made all the decisions herself. "If I tried to do this when he as alive, I'd never hear the end of it."

She wrote the copy for the face of the monument. The stone was treated with an overall green tint. My mother had asked the stonecutter to join us. After our family said several short prayers the stonecutter asked if he could speak a few words.

"I am not telling you anything you cannot see. But in all my years at St. Raymond's I have never seen such a tribute on an original work. Mrs. Toohey, you have showered your husband with the shamrocks of love."

One by one members of the family stepped forward to view our mother's artistry on our father's headstone. The engraving featured my father's name, birth date, date of death and prayerful words In Memoriam. Nowhere was his place of birth mentioned.

The sculpted words were entwined in wreaths of dark green shamrocks flowing across the face of he headstone giving it the suggestion of movement.

We huddled around her with a sense of joy while everyone's eyes filled with tears of sorrow. We left the cemetery quietly and it was a short while before anyone resumed conversation.

Young Laurie broke he silence. "Mom, I thought Daddy was born in the Bronx." Mother remained quiet for several moments before speaking." As I said earlier, I wanted no interference from anyone." She hesitated a few more moments. "I knew you kids wouldn't mind. His friends will be coming to visit his grave. He must have told them hundreds of times that he was born in Ireland, as they all were.

"So I just figured he'd like it. And he'd rest in peace."

Not a word was spoken as we digested the wisdom of our Matriarch.

# Seagram's

## *Mail room*

It was quite a learning experience. I had been hired on as a mail boy at Seagram Distillers duri9ng the summer if 19043 at the age of sixteen. I found that Seagram mail boys deliver letters, memos, and other correspondence to executives behind huge oaken paneled doors that opened to arena sized offices. The inhabitants always spoke in deep dulcet tones, each word carrying the weight of the world. An accompanying rest room, inside the office, was larger than the space allowed for the desk in the low rent departments. Mahogany desks a tad smaller than a professional ice skating rink, where decisions that would challenge the direction of the earth's orbit originated.

The peasants on the lower floor were always busy. They seldom spoke. I later learned 'chatting' was not permitted, unless only on business. Employees were squeezed inside a six by three foot desk area punching numbers incessantly on mechanical Monroe Calculators. I quickly decided that when I grew up I'd prefer the large oaken door that led to the hockey rink. I'd learn to speak in dulcet tones in due time.

We learned to avoid the glare of Horatio who Managed the mailroom with an experienced eye on all us boys. I envisioned being appointed an executive one day and prepared for this eventful day by dressing accordingly. I refused to wear the light tan mail boy jacket made from wrinkled cheesecloth favoring a smart sports jacket. No one complained. I spoke down to my peers and at home to my parents who thought it odd.

This particular mail boy had an eye on his future in business and wouldn't sit behind an archaic desk that housed a pencil pusher many years ago following his tracks to an early grave.

An employee's inevitable destiny begins the moment he or she assumes a sitting position behind an assigned desk. That desk might connect to a link in a master chain that stretches across thirty-nine other desks at that of an authority where rigid rules of passage have been ordained. Stamps of approval must accompany each credit score, inventory confirm, reject slip, accept slip, shipping report and serial number of each qualifying order. Approvals pass link-to- link to a final destination eleven desks in the other direction for another stamp of approval.

Hundreds of employees have been seated at these desks, some for extended periods as long as forty years before being ordained bowing and licking the boots of the hierarchy before retiring to an early grave.

As a worker in the Seagram mailroom during summer session I never ceased to be astonished that young, healthy men of a certain age set their destiny with a billing department and were overjoyed to be retained as a link in a tense and taxing hour-to-hour, day to day singular task perhaps for the rest of their lives.

So much for what I vowed never to do. I thought I'd like to get into advertising. I started in advertising and never left.

I became a budget clerk in the office of the Seagram Advertising Department. From advertising space sales to major positions at the hugest levels of management -- trade publications, newspapers, magazines and the associated creative disciplines of copywriting - sales promotion, and sales managing-- I cared less than a feather or a fig to join another profession.

The mailroom gave me passage to another world of accomplished people in their own rite. The first time I met a handsome, pure white crop of hair and congeniality who was executive finance officer of the entire Seagram distillery. He simply asked me to enter his office in his secretary's absence for a small chat, as they say. I was honored.

There were many other chance meetings with men who had already ascended to the highest ranks of achievement. If not for that exposure the only other place to meet those men would have been through the artificial impressions made by lesser men who merely played the part.

Mr. J.G. Friel many decades later became the leading finance person in the alcoholic beverage industry. "J.G"'s reputation preceded him wherever he went. I was pleased to have met him early on.

I even called him "J.G."

# A Creative Knockout

When I wasn't bored or buried in budget work, I performed "police work" – I'd go on the lookout for those publications that disregarded Seagram's strict no-nonsense rules for ad positioning. Every magazine had to furnish advertisers with "checking copies" to confirm that the advertiser's ad was indeed in the issue and the ad position was as ordered. Most magazines had ad position preferences outlined in stone and magazines sweated through the make-up of each issue to accommodate. There were occasions when I thought the page position of the ad took on greater importance than whether or not the ad ran in the first place.

Certain ad positions were acceptable, others were not. To wit: an ad positioned on the inside front cover, as long as there was no premium charge, was always appreciated; advertising positioned in the front of the magazine, within the first ten pages, on a right hand page, opposite a full page of editorial, was acceptable; for a magazine to position an ad on a right hand page that faced another ad on a left hand page was the equivalent of media suicide. Sales representatives of those offending magazines, God help them, often stayed away from the client's office until things "cooled down."

If a two-page spread was ordered, the center spread position was highly favorable. The next best position would be in the far front of the publication immediately preceding or following the Table of Contents. An ad positioned in the back half of the magazine was no way for a magazine to endear itself to an advertiser. The back cover position always satisfied the client providing no premium was charged. When in doubt, the ad would be positioned on a right hand page, opposite a full page of editorial content, somewhere in the front half of the book (while make-up prayed that he gave 'em what they wanted).

Making up an issue, with ads and editorial not only co-existing but intermingling, was not unlike trying to establish peace in the Middle East, even in the 1950's. Veteran publishing execs told fabricated stories to susceptible junior staffers, of make-up men suffering heart attacks or nervous breakdowns, collapsing over their work tables, defeated by unreasonable positioning demands. From the advertiser's point of view, position was everything in life.

After checking ad positions in Life, Look, Colliers and other leading magazines, I'd turn to the specialty publications – mostly programs for special events that took place in legitimate theaters and sporting arenas, sites where affluent people congregated – where Seagram found it advantageous to place advertising. I came upon the Boxing Programs that were sold and distributed to patrons at Madison Square Garden in New York. Seagram placed a full-page black and white ad for Seven Crown in the Programs.

Upon checking through the Boxing Program, I was surprised that the total page count was almost minimal – not a healthy situation – the equivalent of a feeble person on the verge of collapse. Pages devoted to relevant editorial content seemed scant. Editorial space allotted to profiles of the fighters in each of the programs also appeared inadequate. I noted that there were very few other advertisers in the Boxing Programs – which alone could serve as a death knell. These were all no-nos in the business. In essence, the Boxing Program looked like weak advertising media buys to me but I decided not to forward my criticism to Mr. Clarke. My desire to remain gainfully employed always won out since it was my boss who bought all advertising media, including the Programs.

The Seagram Seven Crown ad looked kind of drab – probably a reflection of the Program itself. The ad said nothing, literally, just a plain old Seven with a Crown on top – no copy, nothing to read – and it wasn't even in a preferred position. I never met the advertising representative from Madison Square Garden Publications and I wondered if he ever made a sales call on Mr. Clarke. Our sad Seven Crown ad got me thinking.

As long as Seagram continued to advertise in the Boxing Programs, I would design a new ad. The ad would be superior to what was running now – could hardly be worse. I thought of the politics, if any, of which I knew nothing. Would I step on anyone's toes? What would Mr. Clarke think? Writing ads was not my responsibility – I was a budget person. Suppose I embarrassed the Warwick & Legler agency and my ad was better than theirs? What would Mr. Moseley have to say to his agency of long standing?

It took me no more than a hasty moment to clear any doubts in my head. I wanted to write the ad regardless and threw all caution to the wind. I must confess, all I really thought about once I decided to move on it, ?? the attention I'd receive from a job well done. But first things first – I'd have to write the ad.

I went into the media library and looked through back issues of Madison Square Garden  Boxing Programs over previous years. They looked identical to the ones I had just checked. The die was cast. Seagram Seven Crown needed a new Boxing ad.

I decided to show a boxing ring with a tall Seven Crown illustration smack in the middle of the ring, kind of like a champion. So far, the ad already looked better than what we were running. And then what, I thought? No need for a paragraph of copy. All I needed was a headline, or a one-liner beneath the boxing ring. That's what I had to think up.

I almost thought of calling a copywriter at Warwick & Legler for ideas but then realized that would be ridiculous! Here I am challenging the agency, granted, in my own small way, but nonetheless. That would be out of the question. As time went on, I thought about copy ideas, while I was in the office, in the subway, at lunch, everywhere. I cam up with nothing. Late one afternoon a stroke of genius hit me right between the eyes, like a prizefighter in a boxing ring. I had the line! I wanted to sketch it into my layout and have someone look at it right away. No way that was going to happen with Mr. Clarke sitting several paces away from me.

Miss Larsen and I by now had gone to lunch a couple of times. We became friends. A Nedick's hot dog and an Orangeade were about all my budget could handle. That was okay wit her. I happened to mention my Boxing Program project to her. She wanted to see it. I thought the best place to do it without attracting outsiders would be to stay after Mr. Clarke went home., that way there would be no distraction.

Once the staff left the office and the cleaning women appeared, Doris and I got together in my office. We sat down at Mr. Clarke's desk. I removed several layouts from my briefcase and took her through my initial rough layout to the final ad showing everything but the copy line.

"Where's the line you thought up?" she asked. I said I was holding it for dramatic effect. She laughed. Then I slid the finished layout before her. It carried the long, awaited line of copy:

# GOOD TO THE LAST ROUND!

She thought it was outstanding. I thought it was outstanding. We both left and took the subway home.

I wondered how I'd get it to one of the agency guys, or maybe even Mr. Moseley himself. Doris suggested she'd just place it on Mr. Moseley's desk when she opened his office in the morning so that he'd see it first thing. I thought that was a bit abrupt and also what about Mrs. Palmer, chummy as she was?

"I can always slide it in with the mail after Mrs. P. gives it to me to bring into to Mr. Moseley." Doris was a jewel. But again, it seemed a bit awkward.

"Maybe you should give it to Mrs. Palmer. Have her show it to Mr. Moseley," I said.

"I can do that," said Doris. I thought twice.

"I don't think that's a good idea. She's liable to just make a comment and then hand it back to you. Then what'll I do?" I let is rest for a while.

Toward the end of the week, I came upon, Roy, the agency exec, during the afternoon. He was going into Mr. Moseley's office with more new layouts. I wished one of them was mine.

"Hi, Marty. What's new?"

"I wrote an ad, Roy." I just spit the words out – almost unintentionally.

"You did? Good for you. Who's your client?"

"Don't laugh, Roy."

"Tell me."

"It's a Seagram ad. I revised the ad we're running in the Madison Square Garden Boxing Programs."

"I'd like to see it. But not now. I've got some business to do. Let me see if I can get down to look at it later."

"What about Mr. Clarke, I asked?" I felt he'd understand my rationale for asking.

"I think you should show it to him first. See what he thinks." I told him I would and I did.

It took Roy a day or two to get around to me but he did drop down to see my ad. I had already shown it to Mr. Clarke who didn't seem impressed one way or the other.

"Everybody wants to be creative," he said. I ignored him.

When I showed it to Roy he had several suggestions but said that the ad made sense. He was going to show it to Mr. Moseley the next day, along with some other stuff. He kept his word.

The next morning, Mr. Moseley came into our office holding my ad. I didn't know what to say. I just froze.

"I like your boxing program idea, Marty." There was that sharp, penetrating tone I always heard coming through his office door that made him sound angry but he wasn't angry. "Roy showed it to me. I told the agency to go ahead with it. Congratulations. You're a pretty good copywriter." I could have floated out the fifteenth floor window and never felt a thing.

Two months later, I saw my ad in the Boxing Program while I was checking copies of magazines. I called Doris and we had a beer to celebrate. You can't party over Orangeade.

# STORES MAGAZINE

H.O. Bell sat behind a long cigar, his bald dome-like head gleaming in Friday's noonday sun. He always looked like he was sneering but I didn't take it personally. His words seemed to be forced out of his mouth between a curled lip and an overlapping nose. A caricaturist would have a field day with that face.

H.O. Bell was Marketing Director of Stores Magazine. I was sitting before him to gain employment. I wanted to be a magazine advertising sales representative and this was the only interview I could get. Stores was owned by the National Retail Dry Goods Association, better known throughout New York's garment center as the NRDGA.

The department store industry read Stores but like any trade publication, it was unknown outside its own industry. If Mr. Bell hired me, I'd likely spend the rest of my time explaining what Stores was. Time, Life and Look preceded their sales reps that hardly needed an introduction.

I had been in my fourth year at Seagram's, approaching my twenty-second birthday. I wanted to start selling magazine advertising instead of listening to others.

I hadn't even gotten the job, yet I was struggling to explain who I worked for.

What does it pay, they asked? Money is seldom mentioned at these higher levels, I'd respond. I've watched dozens of magazine reps call on Mr. Clarke. I knew how to sell.

Mr. Bell asked if I could return the following Friday. The timing worked out well since I had informed Seagram's that I'd be leaving that next Friday.

H.O. Bell was still sitting behind his cigar, when I returned. He was squeezing out words between that curled lip and an over-hanging nose. Aside from his new tie and shirt he could have been implanted one week prior.

He told me that the staff, each of whom was more than twice my age, seasoned independent sales people. I sensed they were professional fund raisers for large charities. They raised money from wealthy philanthropists and corporate leaders and were paid a commission.

During this second interview, H.O. Bell talked of his sales staff and how well they did financially. H.O. Bell led me to believe tat the Stores job could pay one hundred dollars a week, which got my full attention. I was being paid forty dollars a week at Seagram's. One hundred dollars seemed to me to be all the money anyone could possibly earn in one week's time.

"It's a simple equation," he said with great conviction. The more you sell, the more you make. Your colleagues sitting outside do quite well." Dollar signs began to spiral in my head. I shook H.O. Bell's hand and left his office on a cloud. The part-time sales staff's eyes followed me out the door. I sensed jealousy before I even met them.

I came out of the subway and saw a construction gang tearing up Third Avenue. Jackhammers had the sound the Normandy invasion. I felt sorry for the guys pushing down on the hydraulics their bodies shaking in tempo. Would they still shake during dinner with the wife and kids? My God! I felt so lucky. I felt so rich. with the family? Only a few hours left before returning. Sorry to say, I thought of the one hundred dollars a week I would be paid.

Why am I paid more than they do? Why work so hard for less. I felt rich.

The one hundred dollar salary was already going to my head.

When I returned to Mr. Clarke's office I told him how much my new job paid I imagined I made more than Mr. Clarke.

I felt honored at my farewell party. I was given a luxurious leather r briefcase to use in my new position. I felt it was in keeping with someone earning one hundred dollars per week.

During the next two weeks I told everyone of my good fortune. I charged the cost of a new herringbone topcoat with raglan sleeves at the fashionable John David clothing store. A pair of leather gloves, the first I ever owned, and a brown fedora with a yellow feather in the band, topped off my new wardrobe. I felt I could now afford the purchase on my new salary and would pay the balance in full when I picked up the merchandise.

The day I was to start finally arrived. I arrived before nine; Mr. Bell arrived at ten and ignored me. He eventually called me into his office while handing me more account cards. I guessed he had thought, in retrospect, that he didn't give me enough account cards the first time.

"There's no need for you to keep regular office hours since you're an independent rep, as discussed. You can come and go as you please," he said. "The more you sell, the more you make." His words were squeezed out of the natural sneer on his face. They had trouble forcing their way into my brain.

"I don't understand," was the best I could come up with.

"You're independent, not payroll. I thought I mentioned that to you. That you'd be working on commission, not salary. The more you sell, the more you make. You could make one hundred dollars, more or less." I felt trapped inside a tunnel that was filling with water.

I no longer had a job. I had a retail balance coming due. My mother, already struggling, would have even less to pay household bills. For the first time in my life, there was no turning back.

I found an empty chair and joined Stores' sales staff. They were still speaking of the way it was. Boasting about what once was; the jobs they had. They always talked about tomorrow. The promise of tomorrow.

I didn't have a promise to my name.

*　*　*　*　*　*　*　*

My understanding mother offered her full support. I was relieved of my weekly stipend for "room and board" until further notice. I had two options. I could look for another job or report to H.O Bell and try to make a go of it at Stores. I chose the latter.

On the first call I made, I found myself in the sales reception area of a store called, Little Miss Muffit, a children's apparel company, located in the garment center. I listened for my name to be called over the loud speaker. The salesmen I sat with were called vendors. I preferred to be called a sales rep. Vendor sounded like I was selling hot dogs. I spoke with several of the vendors before I realized they were not selling advertising. They were selling patterns, fashions, and buttons, even buttonholes.

"Buttons?" I asked. "Who buys buttons?"

He told me that Little Miss Muffit makes 30,000 coats of three different styles for little girls. "Each style has ten buttons on it, he said. There was no need for me to do the math. When I told him that I was selling advertising in Stores Magazine, he looked non-plussed. Suddenly, buttons seemed like an easier way to make a living. The receptionist's voice blared through the corner speaker every few minutes.

Sy Dorfman. Mr. Weiss will see you now........
Murray Flax. Mr. Cohen will see you now........
Art Edelstein. Mr. Jacobs will see you now........
Marty Ostrow. Mr. Lichtman will see you now........
My name was finally called........
Marty Toohey. Mr. Horowitz will see you now.

Every vendor in the room turned to see what I looked like. Not only was I the youngest in the room I was the only Gentile.

Mr. Horowitz greeted me with a questioning smile. Looking perplexed, he took my business card and asked why I was calling on him. As I tried to explain, he realized that I was not only young and raw but I was wasting my time and his.

"The advertising we do is called co-op advertising. We advertise to the public in newspapers like the Herald Tribune – under the name of the department store we are cooperating with. We then share the cost of the ad. But the ad runs under the Macy's or Gimbels name. Our products appear in their ad." I felt as though I was getting a lesson in Advertising 101, which I was.

"You might want to call on the larger firms that advertise directly to department stores. Your magazine would be useful for that." My very first sales call resulted in a short lesson in retail advertising. I guessed that if this were typical of the sales calls I'd be making, I'd wind up very smart, but very poor.

Everything about my new position was strange to me. The neighborhood was heavy with the hustle and bustle of trucks carrying tomorrow's. The crosstrees were no longer in numerical order as in uptown. I returned to Stores. H.O. Bell was in his glass-paneled office with the door closed. The independent reps were reading the newspapers. They seemed to be waiting for someone to call. If one referred to a chairman of the board as "a close friend," l the others would say, almost in unison, "I know him, too."

I struck up a conversation with the middle-aged woman who always wore her hat in the office. She dressed very business-like but came across cold and snippy.

"And what brings you to Stores young man?" Her name was McDonald. I gave her a short outline of my years at Seagram's but little else.

"I should think that you'd join a publication with a sales training program rather than being thrown to the wolves, if you don't mind my saying so. Which accounts do you intend calling on?" I sensed that I shouldn't answer that question. The woman's son sat alongside her. He appeared to be a short young man in his middle twenties or older. He wore a bright handkerchief in the breast pocket of his topcoat. He introduced himself and joined the conversation. As he pulled up a chair, his mother spoke. "This young man intends to sell business into Stores magazine, William, without any training and without any accounts that have value." William responded in the same snippy tone as his mother. "Lotsa luck!" he said laughing.

"My son and I live in the Murray Hill section of Manhattan, a very high class neighborhood. We're in the same building as many celebrities. The singer Fran Warren lives on the floor beneath us but we live way up on the thirty-fifth floor. She made it sound as though anyone living beneath the thirty-fifth floor may as well be living in the street. I told her I lived in the Bronx, which got no recognition.

"I sell the lion's share of business in Stores Anniversary Issue," she continued. Mr. Bell appeared and called for me to come into his office. He closed the door and proceeded to preach to me. "I must warn you to stay away from Mrs. McDonald and her son, William. They're bad characters. Untrustworthy. They'll steal your accounts one by one and you'll never know it until one of them turns up on the billing sheet. Then it's too late." I was a bit startled at H.O. Bell's descriptions.

"Did she tell you they live in Murray Hill and that a popular singer lives in the same building?" Did she tell you they bring in most of the business in Stores?"

I answered yes on all accounts.

"All lies!" Last month she had trouble paying her rent in that fancy apartment of hers. Don't don't pay any attention to her. She asked me for another advance and I turned her down. She hasn't paid the first one back.

"They'll probably dine in some fancy hotel tonight. William will sign the check and list a phony room number as usual. Momma has taught him all the tricks."

I became more familiar with the business and began to search out account names to solicit for H.O. Bell's approval. After six weeks or so, H.O. Bell handed me the Steinway & Sons account, much to my surprise. I didn't even know department stores sold pianos. I got an appointment with a John Steinway whom I imagined was probably ten years old. H.O. Bell would not have trusted me calling on an adult person with the legendary Steinway name. But that's what he did.

I had a pleasurable meeting with John Steinway who advised me that Steinway buys the special issue of Stores every year. He signed a contract; I presented it to H.O. Bell who responded in kind.

"You'll soon be here six weeks and it's time we changed your deal," he said. "You will now be in a position to earn commissions over and above a forty-dollar salary. I think you'll do very well and I think your mother will be pleased."

The gods must have been listening. Only two months earlier I expected to be paid one hundred dollars per week only to be crushed to learn I had real it all wrong. Now an offer of less than half that amount still put me in the same joyous frame of mind. I was earning income again. I wanted to shout the news to every truck grinding through the garment center.

The new payment plan didn't work out as H.O. Bell thought it would. He never registered disappointment in me. I continued to make the sales calls day in, day out, but sold very little. It was indeed time for a change. I was mismatched. At first I thought it was me. Years later I realized that magazines are a lot like people. In the cold hard world of advertising, the maxim, what have you done for me lately? holds true for magazines as well. After scanning through back issues of tStores, I decided the editorial content hadn't done anything for anybody save three or four losers who continued to earn commissions for a month or two each year.

Earlier the N.Y. Times had offered me a job selling classified advertising. I spoke with the manager of that department. His name was Darling D. Darling. I assumed his middle initial stood for another Darling but was afraid to ask. I used a Mr. before his last name each time I addressed him lest anyone within earshot got the wrong idea. He outlined the job assignment for me.

"Are you suggesting I make sales calls on little old ladies looking to unload a broken old phonograph player or moth-eaten couch through an ad in your newspaper?" I asked. I sensed a smile in his voice when he responded.

"Not quite, Mr. Toohey. Your sales category will include the many commercial advertisers we carry – businessmen wanting to sell their furniture from a company they might be closing; or selling tons of heavy industrial equipment from plants here in New York to buyers elsewhere. Remember, there is a buyer for everything.

"We don't call on little old ladies, or even little old men. They call us when they have things to sell."

When I learned it would take a year or more before I'd be calling on large display advertisers – department stores, major retail outlets and the like, with a future in selling national advertising, I told him I was no longer interested.

I had worn out my welcome calling on the N.Y. newspapers and newsmagazines. I did not have enough experience.

The Jersey Journal, a Jersey City newspaper, ran a want ad in the N.Y. Times for an "advertising sales representative," not a "vendor," which in itself was promising. I'd be selling to retailers including some of the major department stores. It seemed like a good opportunity to get into the sales side of the business with an eye on eventually returning to New York. I passed the interview process and after considering the daily commute from the Bronx to Jersey City that was long but reasonable, I decided I'd cross the river.

Unlike Stores, there wasn't a person, at least in Jersey City, who didn't know what the

Jersey Journal was. To my inquisitive friends I said, "It's a major newspaper. Just like] the Daily News." That held them until they discovered we didn't carry Dick Tracy

# MOLONEY'S MEAT MARKET

Moloney had flaming red hair on top of a face covered with freckles. His profile resembled that of an eagle in flight, squinty eyes and large hooked nose leading the way. He spent a good part of each day almost suspended in motion inside his butcher shop, leaping from the giant refrigerator to his showcase of fine cut meats, hardly touching the floor. He'd hop over to the cash register once he wrapped the meat and then serve the customer. In 1957, I was the advertising representative for the Jersey Journal, the only newspaper in town. I picked up his copy each week. I always had to wait until there were no customers in his store. The two of us would then discuss his next week's ad. This was a Tuesday, the usual day I picked up his items and the prices. His store was crowded each time I stopped by so I called to him to let him know that I'd be back on Wednesday in plenty of time to make the Thursday edition when most food ads ran.

Moloney's advertisement in the newspaper measured approximately ten inches tall by two columns wide. The ad carried four items positioned in horizontal boxes with one large box at the top reserved for the special of the week. "Make certain you position my ad at the top of the page! It was on the bottom of the page last week and almost ruined my business. I was practically stuck with a ton of corned beef!" I took everything he complained about with a grain of salt. Every one of my advertisers wanted their ads to appear at the top of the page except for those who ran a full page ad and they wanted their ad to appear on page three of the newspaper. "Put it on the first right hand page. That's the page they turn to the most." I empathized with the advertisers since I felt that ads given preferential positioning managed to be more effective than those that appeared on a page with five or six other ads.

Mr. Stern, manager of Acme Appliances, seemed to know this. "I don't run a full page ad every week, so make sure this gets beneficial treatment." One would think that any ad appearing in the back of the newspaper was the end of the world. "You know where the good spots are in your paper. Keep my ad away from the church listings and the obituaries. Anyone reading the obituaries is not in the mood to buy a washer and dryer. They're thinking of flowers for the grave sit, and I don't sell flowers, so keep me away from the obituaries."

As soon as the store had emptied out, I walked behind the display case and sat down with Moloney to discuss next week's ad: "Price lamb chops at 49 cents; pork chops, 39 cents; chopped meat, 16 cents; and t-bone steaks, 64 cents. Put those items in the four boxes the way we always do. Do you have pictures of the four cuts? We've run them before. You should still have them." I took notes as he spoke. Newspapers subscribed to a Mat Service that carried pictures of just about every known product. The salesmen at the newspaper cut out the drawing of the item and glued it in the ad. The composing room would be given the picture, select the corresponding mat and pour molten lead on a cardboard replica of the drawing and a printing plate would be made. I wrote down the prices of each of the four items.

"The special this week will be a rib roast. Make it as large as you can but leave room for the price that I also want large. I'm giving it a special price so treat this ad special. It's priced at 69 cents." Moloney wanted all of his prices to be bold and large with heavy black lettering but like most other advertisers, he didn't want to increase the size of his ad. "How am I going to run a larger ad if your publisher keeps increasing the advertising rates!" There was no way of getting around Moloney's dissatisfaction with everything and anything that Jersey Journal did. I never received a thank you or a compliment on the appearance of the ad. He probably figured I'd take advantage and suggest he run an even bigger ad.

Once back in the office, I proceeded to sort out the notes, sketches and advertising copy picked up during the sales calls I had made that day. There was Moloney's copy on top. I roughed it out, selected the pictures for requiring mats and sent it upstairs to the composing room. Upstairs knew his ads even better than I did. I laid out the other ads I had in my bag, sent them to composing and left for home.

The following day on Wednesday, when proofs came down, the Moloney proof was missing. I called the composing room to check on it and for whatever reason I learned that the ad had not even been cast in lead as yet. This would l eave no time to deliver proofs. I didn't see this as a catastrophe. The newspaper would more than likely provide a proof later in the day. I went about my business. The next morning when the Thursday edition came out there was Moloney's ad in the upper right hand corner on a right hand page. It made my day.

Around ten o'clock that morning my telephone rang. The voice on the other end was impossible to decipher. Someone was ranting and screaming. When he had settled down I recognized Moloney's voice.

"Did you see my ad this morning? Have you seen the mistake in the price? Do you have any idea of what this will cost me?" By this time I had turned to the page that carried Moloney's ad. I saw nothing to warrant his hysterical reaction. Fishing around for my notes, I finally found them. I quickly discerned the reason for Moloney's hysteria. The price of chopped meat had been transposed with the price of his rib roast. Rib roasts were now priced at 16 cents a pound. Customers would be jamming his meat market. I almost laughed, but stifled it. There was more hysteria and more shouting from Moloney who not only wanted the newspaper to credit him for the ad but to offset whatever losses he would suffer from the mistake. Allowing Moloney to settle down I told him I would see that he received satisfactory treatment for this unfortunate error.

I walked slowly to our advertising manager's desk and reported the mistake to him. His initial response was to ask if Moloney had approved a proof of the ad. Then he suggested a twenty percent reduction in the cost of the ad that allows for the space used in the rib roast mistake. When I explained the dire situation and the raving behavior of the butcher he seemed more understanding. Finally, it was agreed that the newspaper would provide a letter that would explain the transposition in prices.

The newspaper would take the blame for the mistake due to an error. Moloney would also receive full credit for the ad. When I delivered the letter, he wouldn't even look at me. Instead, he snatched the letter from my hand, read it, and pasted it on a wall for everyone to see. Moloney then addressed a number of women who were clamoring for rib roast at sixteen cents per pound. When I left, Moloney was pointing to the letter for all to see before tending to the growing swarm of customers. He was no longer in suspended animation. Every customer in the store that demanded a rib roast at 16 cents a pound had to be shown the letter of explanation.

Unfortunately, once word got out about the long lines outside Moloney's every advertiser demanded the upper right hand corner on page three. There could be only one upper right hand corner on page 3 available. Logic tells us this. I could not get grown men to understand. Obviously, it was an assignment for my boss, Jim Wear. We must make bosses earn their keep, whenever possible. The merchants were still screaming at him as I drove by.

# BILLBOARD

## I Call On The East Coast

But what will you say?

After two years at the Jersey Journal, I joined Billboard Publishing, a music industry trade paper noted for its authoritative Billboard Top 100, the "bible" of the music industry.

I thought I'd be assigned several major record label accounts. I'd become a hot shot Top 100 sales rep and hang out with Johnny Mathis, Tony Bennett and Steve and Edie, who were at the top of the charts. Tom Noonan, my high school friend for life, set up appointments for me with Billboard management.

Tom's duties included, among other things, complete control of The Top 100. I'm certain he helped me get hired. I was appointed manager of the coin machine mad jukebox sections. It was as dull as dust.

I called on the drones of Tenth Avenue, made conversation with coin machine distributors who worked out of storefronts on Tenth Avenue that looked like they were condemned. They led millionaire lifestyles because most were already millionaires. . They didn't believe in advertising, because they had the juke box operators, their prime client base, in their nip pocket.

Billboard's salesmen would have lasted about an hour-and-a-half trying to keep up with the sales pace at the Jersey Journal. We made more sales calls in a single day than they did in a week.

Billbord salesmen, all except me, sold advertising in Vend Magazine and were located in the coin machine offices with jukebox guys like me.

Vend guys never left the office. While I was rarely in tithe office, the sales force seemed to read vending journals and the trade papers all day long .Ron Carpenter was the eastern ad manager of Vend Magazine. He was also the ad manager of me. What he knew about coin machines could slide through the coin slot of a jukebox with room to spare.

After I made weekly sales calls on Tenth Avenue, the hub of jukebox industry in NYC and Philadelphia's Broad St. where those multi-millionaire distributors also found no value in advertising.

One morning I told Ron who was still my ad manager, that I'd like to branch out and start calling on coin machine distributors on the east coast -- from Miami to Maine.

He told me the sales force only made long distance telephone calls once each year when the new models were introduced. . I remember Ron asking me, "What are you going to say once you get there?" I suddenly wanted to tell Ron about a sales opening he might apply for with the competition.

I did gain permission to open the east coast. I retained the services of an excellent travel agent named Gertie. "Hey, Gert.

I'm going to Atlanta next week. Where should; I stay?" She was excellent. "Atlanta? Stay at the brand new Renaissance on Peachtree Street. The elevators are visible from inside at the center of the massive lobby. They run up and down the sides of the tower in the center. You can see the people inside as far up as the 30th floor.

Gertie knew everything. "Oh," she added." Do not stay at the Embassy, which used t to be our favorite hotel." She told us an opera singer either jumped or was pushed off her 23rd floor terrace. The Atlanta police have one guess. They say she may have hit one too many clunkers during rehearsal that afternoon singing the duet from "Vista La Juba." I asked her what that had to do with the tragedy. "They say the maestro is very finicky about pitch," " said Gertie.

* * * * * * * *

I called on every distributor from Miami to Maine. I'd take off every week or two then check back in on Tenth Avenue and Broad Street in Philly when I returned. I forget the percent I increased the ad linage but it was considerable.

After two years, the east coast was solid, business was never better, and it was time for an accounting -- from the payroll department.

Pay increase time came around and to my astonishment, we all got the same increase. The guys who left the office to take a pee, the trade paper bookworms and the guys who never missed going to lunch with each other. Then there was me who spent half the year in towns like Tecumseh, S.C.; and Variarible, DE; and Intercourse, MI. fighting and almost wrestling for every scrap of advertising space from the wholesalers.

I called Hilmer Stark, my national manager located in Chicago, to let him know of my bitter disappointment.

"Marty, I know how you must feel. We'll make it up to you next time. "

"There's not going to be a next time, Hilmer. Once is enough."

Dick Ford called from Chicago. Dick was my immediate superior and one of my favorite people.

"Mart, give me a chance to make it up to you. Let's have you travel to New England on business each week, with the family, in the summer, as often as you desire, and let us pick up the tab to have you stay over at your favorite resort – Cape Cod- all on the house. Take from Friday morning to Monday afternoon."

I couldn't believe my ears.

"Dick, I know you want what's best for me. But Hilmer stands in our way. "Thank you for coming to my aid Dick, but no thanks"

I called Perry Wachtel wino owned DePerri Advertising Agency.

"Perry, this is Marty Toohey. I understand you're looking for a new account executive."

"Your timing couldn't be better, Marty," he said.

"Glad to hear it. Can we talk? "

# CASH BOX

## Tenth Avenue, Mettallic Suits

The FBI called

Tenth Avenue was a bus ride from the Madison Avenue ad biz but in reality more than a planet away. It was on the west side of town, one block from the Hudson River, perfect for drowning people.

Coin machine row, as it was referred to in the trade, housed one dozen coin machine distributors on a fifteen block stretch. I spent more years than I care to remember on Tenth Avenue selling ad space for Billboard; as an account exec for the DePerri ad agency; writing a weekly column and selling ad space for Cash Box; and finally as a regional Vice President for the Seeburg Corporation. That's an eleven year involvement in the juke box business which was hardly my chosen profession. I guess one could say I mismanaged my career for a decade successful agency noted for its outstanding creative approach to marketing top brands – Coke, Camels, Proctor and Gamble, Chrysler – all household names, products bought by the masses.

Here I was about to re-enter a world of metallic suits and cuff links the size of melons and for what? For money, that's what. Working with jukebox distributors on one side of town while continuing to dream of having success in the advertising business on the other side, required a mental straddle that almost split my pants.

Cash Box called me in 1958. They knew me from my work at the DePerri ad agency and Billboard. I jumped at the Cash Box offer to double my salary. It was not the first of several missteps I made in pursuit of a successful advertising career. In the interest of those who may not finish this book, you should know that my exit from Cash Box, seven years later, was just as suicidal. I was the guy in the cartoon who walks out the window of a high rise but doesn't plummet to the ground until realizes he's walking on thin air. I jumped at the money – again, and then again several years later and I found myself crawling on this air – again.

Cash Box served an untidy coin machine industry made up of dubious operator contracts, cash boxes spilling over with nickels and dimes, popular 45-rpm recordings and the artists who made them, and a national industry movement referred to as " dime play," intended to double the intake of those nickels and dimes. Instead of continuing to forge ahead inside the sophistication of the advertising business, I chose to sell large ads to small businessmen where refinement was at a premium. It was an ill-considered move. But it paid twice the money.

Coin machine row was a succession of coin-operated businesses that started at 42nd Street and Tenth Avenue and ran north to Fifty-seventh Street with about twelve distributors spread out along fifteen blocks. I walked north each Tuesday afternoon, and solicited advertising materials for ads to run in Cash Box. Four dealers on the avenue sold competing brands of jukebox models – Seeburg, Rock-Ola, AMI and Wurlitzer. Others sold various lines of coin-operated pinball machines and shuffle alley games made by Williams, United, Gottlieb and Bally Manufacturing, the same Bally of today's Las Vegas and national health club fame.

I was manager of the coin machine department of the magazine which meant that I sold advertising to distributors and manufacturers based in New York, and to other coin machine firms along the east coast with regular sales trips between Buffalo and Miami.

"Eastern Flashes," was a business gossipy column that I wrote each week, inserting pretty much the same names but in different settings. How else you gonna write about the same fifteen, twenty guys without seeming to repeat yourself? Writing frivolous folksy news items on Thursdays based on the same people I called on the previous Tuesday, was a trial. The trade, nonetheless, read it regularly, and as best I could determine, took it seriously. I was what I liked to think of, laughingly, as a two-fisted journalist, probably the only advertising guy who also wrote supportive editorial for his clients.

Barney Sugarman excited about the new 1960 AMI model jukebox just introduced at his distributorship. Looks like another successful model year for Shugy. . . . .Abe Simon, United Distribs, back from Miami in time to promote his new shuffle alley game, Black Jack. . . . .Word on the street has it that the transition from a nickel a tune to "dime play" on the nation's juke boxes is gathering steam. . . . .Al "Senator" Bodkin, everyone's favorite operator, still spreading his brand of humor during his weekly visits to coin machine row. . . . .etc.

\*     \*     \*     \*     \*     \*     \*     \*

Mike Manves was an exception to the traditional distributor on Tenth Avenue. He sold coin operated amusement machines to penny arcades— fortune telling equipment, card trick games – the same kind kids played on fifty years before and in Mike's case, probably the same machines, restored ten or more times over the years. Mike Munves had a monopoly on the arcade market since the 1950's. The machine manufacturers had long since gone out of business and Mike had cornered the market by buying up the dyes, parts, whatever the factory could ship him at a fraction of the cost.

Everything in the Munves place of business, including Mike himself, was ancient. The "showroom" consisted of dozens of dusty old machines that stood like monuments in a graveyard. Doll-like figures, dressed in tuxedos or gypsy costumes, moved in animated fashion to eerie music inside glass enclosures. Dolls dressed up as royalty, dealt cards to each other. Others told fortunes, in exchange for a penny – and issued fortune-telling cards that promised nothing but good news to the optimistic winner.

\*     \*     \*     \*     \*     \*     \*     \*

After calling on Mike, either for an ad in Cash Box or a bit of gossip that went into my column, I'd hustle along to Runyon Distributors, one block away. Runyon was the official AMI juke box distributor in the New York metropolitan area. It was owned by Barney Sugarman, better known as "Shugy," a pleasant sort of fellow who was powerful I was told, for reasons that had to do with his business associates and inside investors. I never did see any tangible evidence that Shugy dealt from the bottom of the deck until the day he died. We waited outside the synagogue and stood with a large crowd. A long line of Fleetwood Cadillacs, all customized Brougham models, featuring the latest in vinyl roof covering, with a decorative chrome handle behind each rear side window, were parked outside. The luxury sedans would be driven by their owners, behind Shugy's hearse, on the way to the cemetery. Some flack, standing with another group, openly wondered who was left behind to run their illegal gambling operations throughout the State of New Jersey. Apparently there was little concern by the drivers in the fleet, as the Cadillacs followed their friend Shugy inside the hearse into the sunset.

Shugy was diminutive in size even with large Cuban heels attached to his shoes, always impeccably attired, and seldom smiled, except whenever I joined him in his office to discuss a small advertising program in Cash Box.

"What did you say your wife's maiden name was, Marty?"

"Gorman. Maureen Gorman."

"Are you sure it wasn't Goldman?" he kidded. I'd laugh and he'd explain.

"the reason I ask is because you are becoming more Jewish with each passing week making sales calls on us Jews in the coin machine business!" Then we'd both laugh.

"Tell me, when is Joe going to give you a piece of the action?" That's when I wished Shugy was my personal agent.

# SEEBURG

## Sweet Lorraine

Take your press clippings

Cassettes from my tape collection were scattered on the empty passenger seat as I drove west on Rt. 94. I was to report to Jack Gordon, president of Seeburg, one of my Cash B ox advertisers. I had quit Cash Box to take Gordon's offer for twice my salary.

Berrien Springs was just two hours from Chicago. Tony Bennett was singing Sweet Lorraine, a song that had been very special to me for many years.

I had brought along three plastic containers each holding three or four of my favorite tapes. There wasn't a cough in a carload. I reached across to the passenger seat looking for an open plastic box while I drove and removed one tape at random and played it. That's when I heard Tony singing "Sweet Lorraine". I remembered when he recorded it in the 1950's. The soft, warbly clarinet notes behind Tony had to come from Joe Marsala. The recording was filled with a bouquet of memories.

My first recollection of the song took me back to my teenage years, on vacation with the guys at Loon Lake, a resort in the Adirondack Mountains where we played softball, swam, drank beer and picked up girls. I fell in love with "Sweet Lorraine" the moment I heard it introduced by Nat "King" Cole on a juke box that rainy afternoon. I fell in love with Dixie O'Day that night.

We prepped for the Saturday night Loon Lake dance by showering and shaving and splashing Aqua-Velva all over our faces and wherever we thought it would do the most good. My guys warmed up by scanning the room for quail, as they say. Sightings were made. We began to multiply. Our table of four became a table for six and then seven.

I already had my target for tonight. Dixie was the prettiest girl at the dance. Soft brunette hair long before every girl turned blonde, Dixie had what was then called a Pepsodent smile. I could almost smell the toothpaste. She wore shorts, which not every young woman did in those days. Dixie looked gorgeous in heels and mini-shorts that emphasized her legs -- legs that just wouldn't quit. I guessed we were about the same age — seventeen or thereabouts. She was receptive to my invitation to dance. Some say that timing is everything but the Gods of love must have something to do with it, too. How else would the band know to play "Sweet Lorraine" just as we began to dance?

"I love this song," she said.

All I could think to say as my heart pulsated was, "Me, too."

Me, too?!, I thought. Me, too?! Was that all I could say? Me, too?! Monkeys have a vocabulary larger than Me, too! Yet that's all I could spout out.

"Have you heard Nat Cole's version?" she asked. I was not going to repeat those two dumb words again. No more, me-too's, I vowed.

"I heard it this afternoon on the juke box in the pavilion," I said.

"Me, too," she said. But she said it so much nicer than I did.

Dixie O'Day and I became an item that week at Loon Lake. We even kissed a few times. I called her weeks later from our corner drug store on Clay Avenue back in the Bronx. We dated several times. She lived "downtown", which meant Manhattan. I guess I felt it was too long a haul. Maybe I was intimidated although I don't know why after practically spending the week with her. I guess we can blame it on my youth. I thought of Dixie O'Day for the first time in fifty years when I heard Tony singing Sweet Lorraine. She's probably the only seventy-five year old woman in the world who still looks seventeen. I'll bet she doesn't even have gray hair.

\*　　\*　　\*　　\*　　\*　　\*　　\*　　\*

"Sweet Lorraine" came back into my life some twenty odd years later when Jack Gordon hired me to work for Seeburg, the juke box company in Chicago. I sat in Gordon's office during my initial visit to the Chicago plant. I knew Jack as president of Seeburg from my Cash Box Magazine days. Seeburg was one of our largest advertisers.

"You know Joe Marsala," Gordon said expecting me to agree. "We have Joe on the payroll to help develop some ideas I have for our new division, called Seeburg Music."

I didn't know Joe Marsala, I didn't know Seeburg was developing a separate music division, nor did I have any idea of when my orientation would begin.

"Joe's been cutting some records for our new Seeburg dance catalog," said Gordon, referring to a record session that had apparently ended a few minutes ago. "He just called me. Should be here any minute."

I learned that Gordon and Marsala met back in the forties when they were both active in the big band business – Joe playing in New York and around the country with various jazz bands, Gordon working for music publishers.

Joe Marsala, born around the turn of the century, began as a jazz clarinetist. He played in the early 1930's with Dixieland greats from Eddie Condon to Jack Teagarden, and married classical harpist, Adele Gerard.

"Tony called Joe," said Gordon. "He's cutting a new album and wants Joe for one selection on the album. Isn't that great?" he said. "Joe will tell you all about it when he gets here."

"Joe made a recording of 'Sweet Lorraine' many years ago. Bobby Hackett, who plays trumpet on almost all of the selections in Tony's new album, suggested that Tony use Joe. Simple as that."

Gordon's office door opened and a man with a hangdog expression walked in unannounced just as the telephone rang. He picked up the phone and exclaimed, "Here he is. Marty, say hello to Joe Marsala. I have to take this call." He motioned to the two of us to relocate to the conference area of his expansive office. Joe and I sat down at the other side of the room.

I imagined Joe's facial expression resembled that of a Mafia mobster. It was wrinkled, craggy, beat-up, and totally expressionless. Several minutes into our conversation, a bright smile burst through his face. I didn't even realize he had teeth. Joe Marsala's gentle voice surprised me. Marsala sounded like a kind man who didn't have a braggadocio bone in his body.

"You working for Jack," he asked.

"I'm supposed to be working for someone. I've been here for a while but I still don't know what I'm supposed to do. I'm waiting for direction."

"Jack and I go way back even before the Hickory House," he said, without acknowledging my situation.

"He used to stop by almost every night when Adele and I played there." I could see that the conversation turned to recollection of the good old days. I had noticed that performers with a history tend to talk about the days when they were on top. It's sad in a way. However, I thought here's a guy in his mid sixties, has probably been struggling for twenty years, and he's on the Seeburg payroll. Joe seemed secure, at least as long as Jack Gordon was on top, or as long as Joe's wife Adele continued playing.

"Did Jack tell you Tony called me?" Joe asked. Joe was talking to me as if we had known each other for decades. I was surprised Marsala brought it up so soon, almost as though he'd continue to tell the world for as long as he lived. He said it in a way that made him seem so grateful, so appreciative. I guess that when old-timers are remembered, especially by headliners like Tony Bennett, it must give them a wonderful feeling just to be remembered, let alone he asked to perform. This must be the daily conversation at show business rest homes, I thought.

"Tony was here in Chicago with Bobby Hackett. I've known Bobby since he played trumpet as a kid. Tony has Bobby playing horn on his new album. He asked Bobby to talk me into playing 'Sweet Lorraine' on the album," Joe said. "Hell, I haven't played clarinet for ten years. I didn't think I was ready." I was mesmerized listening to Joe Marsala relate a story that I felt was extremely intimate.

"Tony called me. He said he wanted to record the song as a salute to the late Nat Cole. And he wanted me, and only me, to play clarinet behind him. When I told him I felt rusty, Tony said, 'Pour some oil on it. See you in the studio next week.'

"We cut the record last Thursday in one take. Tony loved it. He said to me, 'Hey, Joe. I thought you said you were rusty!'

"Wasn't that nice what he said?' I'll tell you something Marty, I blew it the only way I know how and Tony sang his heart out."

When the Tony Bennett album was released I rushed out to buy it, taped the entire recording and added it to my private collection to be played in my car.

Now here I was, driving west to Chicago, thirty-eight years later, listening to Joe Marsala playing sultry, bluesy notes in the background, Bobby Hackett blowing horn during the introduction and Tony Bennett singing "Sweet Lorraine". I thought of Dixie O'Day.

# ADIOS SEEBURG

## Via Long Distance!

During the winter of 1965 following a seven-day successful sales trip through the frigid north of Buffalo, Syracuse and the others, I was fired from my employment via long distance telephone upon my return. My discharge took place while employed by the Seeburg Corporation where I was a regional sales VP at $20,000 annually when my buddies were earning $10,000, a variance that provided me with the wrong reason to accept the job.

I quickly learned that Seeburg, like families, who spend more than they make, go broke. Seeburg closed the plant and thousands were fired. I was "outta work", the title of my next four chapters. It took that long to re-gain employment.

When I first called Bill Adair, our Vice-Chairman in Chicago who hired me originally, the conversation went something like this:

"Hey, Bill! Just got back from upstate New York. Sold the Seeburg program just the way you taught me, Signed three distributors in four days. Not bad, eh?

Bill – Marty, your services are no longer required by the Seeburg Corporation. Today is your last day. I'll put your severance check in the mail. Good luck.

I remember hearing a click.

Adair's final words sounded as if they were taped. Maybe they were and he played the same song for everyone. I hung up and walked out to the kitchen to give my wife the bad news. We both wondered how much severance pay was on the way and decided to cut back on our Christmas shopping plans for the kids.

Radio news forecasted blizzard-like snow and rain storms on into the remainder of the week. A sorry state of affairs was transportation in New York City. A major subway strike crippled all other modes of transportation -- busses, trucks, passenger cars and taxicabs. Ten million stranded subway riders scattered on the City's streets unable to reach their places of business.

An apt title later defined New York City's crippling disaster: "The Perfect Storm"

# OuttaWork

## Part 1
## I Called Howie

There was a two-week-old subway strike in New York that paralyzed all transportation for those trying to get to their jobs, and for those who wished they had a job to get to.

I managed to garner seventeen job interviews in early December, before the strike, through want ads and personal recommendation. Had my interviews been measured as sales calls I would have qualified again as salesman of the year, a title I was familiar with from previous occasions.

Personnel managers had a prepared statement for getting rid of job applicants. "Call me after the holidays. Maybe we'll have something then."

Some of us in search of employment took the managers at their word. The end result was that the managers found themselves up to their hips with job applicants on January 2, 1966, one day "after the holidays". I turned my back on that feeble offer.

Just before Christmas I was reduced to watching TV during the day, surprised in fact there was something called daytime TV. Who watched TV in the daytime, I wondered? Funny how the unemployed feel that everyone else but them has a job

A television performer named Steve Allen was a quizmaster on an afternoon program. I was watching it of sheer boredom.

I heard him say, "Another mistake we make after we're fired is to keep it a secret." My neighbor's wife had asked me only this morning why I was still home. I believe I said, "Doctor's appointment."" We should but we don't call our friends and tell them we just got fired? You know why?" he continued. "Aha!" he exclaimed." Embarrassment! That's why!"

I reached for the phone and called Howie Friedberg. He had recently joined the Ziff-Davis Publishing Co. He had spoken well of the firm.

Howie said, "You're what? Did you say fired?" He went on and on. "Why would anyone fire Marty Toohey? You are the very best!" He went on blowing my horn. Howie often talked like that and I never saw reason to stop him. Practically very time Howie gave me one of his pep talks; I wanted to ask my boss for a raise.

Howie told me he'd do something he has never done before.

"I'm going straight to Bill Ziff and tell him the best advertising salesman in the world is on the beach!" He said he'd call me after he spoke with Mr. Ziff.

# Part 2
## I take the down elevator

I stood under a store ledge on the corner of 86th Street and Lexington Avenue. A drenching rain had continued since early morning darkness. I had just left another employment agency with nothing but promises in hand.

Normally, I'd be two subway express stops and a five-minute walk to my next appointment, fifty-three blocks away. There was little that was normal about this day, this month, tnis 1965 Christmas season.

I had been fired several weeks earlier. My wife and I cut back on gifts for our five children, the oldest of whom was nine.

There was a two-week-old subway strike in New York that paralyzed transportation for all en route to their jobs, and for those who wished they had a job to struggle to. Even the Christmas carolers standing under an awning outside Bloomingdale's seemed to be singing out of tune.

It's near impossible to gain an employment appointment with Christmas just around the corner. I had reasons to forge ahead, to trudge if not swim to 2 Park Avenue not the least of which might be my final grasp at survival. It was sixty-three blocks away. I prepared to do the breaststroke.

I managed to garner seventeen job interviews in early December err mostly through Want Ads amend cold calls. The silence from interviewers on he opposite side of the desks was deafening. "Come back after New Year's. Maybe we'll have something then."

I guessed they told that to every job seeker. I pictured throngs of the hopeless unemployed were being wedged into every elevator in the lobby. Uniformed starters cramming the remaining job seeker into the imaginary space crushing a gentleman's smart Christmas gift fedora, on the early morning of Monday January 2, 1966. I turned and walked away. It was the first job opportunity I had turned my back on.

Just before Christmas I was reduced to watching TV during the say. I was surprised there was TV during the way. Who watched TV in the daytime? Could there be me and nobody else?

TV buyers mistakenly read the "1" as one million which they were accustomed to seeing. Would their boss question the buy? "Carillon, only lone person watched the TV show you bought. I can't imagine why you bought tins show with only one viewer. Explain please."

So I'm, not only unemployed, I adding to the unemployed ranks by having others fired.

A television performer named Steve Allen was a quizmaster on various programs, including the show I was watching.

I heard him say, "Another mistake we make after we're fired is to keep it secret." My neighbor's wife had asked me this morning as to why I was home. I believe I said, "Doctor's appointment." or "I'll be leaving later." VW was ten minutes away from the freeway to the George Washington Bridge. She accepted my reason.

Steve Allen continued." Why wouldn't you call all your fiends and ell them you lost your job?" I agreed with him. I'd call my friends. "You know why?" "Aha!" he exclaimed." Embarrassment!" That's why!"

I reached for the phone and called Howie Friedberg. He had recently joined Ziff-Davis Publishing and he made the company sound like Heaven.

"You're what? Did you say fired?" He Went on and on. "Why should anyone fire Marty Toohey? You arte the best" He often talked like this and I never, ever saw reason to stop him. Every time Howe gave one of his pep talks, I asked for a raise. Now I'm asking for a job.

# Part 3
# A naked city

The down elevator sped me to the lobby. Small hailstones danced on the streets as if it were a giant playground. The ice chilled warm memories of Ms. Eddy's hot coffee and thoughtfulness. Taxicabs drove by with passengers hanging out the windows, no more room not even for one more customer.

Another cab spun out on Park Avenue, missed hitting a Jeep, and finally came to a stop but now faced oncoming traffic. I was about to cross Park Avenue when two grown men fought over each other's 'rights' to a taxicab trying to unload it passengers.

A middle aged man and an urbane woman were melded in a suggestive position, neither moving a muscle. They couldn't exit their way out until those under them managed to slither from the cab. They did not seem in a hurry.

Women had a disadvantage during the slithering segment since fashions of the 1960's dictated women wear dresses during business hours.

Flash bulbs popped while photogs scampered to focus on the legs and under garments of ladies whose dress might bunch around the collar as they exit. . Intermittent screams of fright from some, sheer ecstasy from others, mixed with the anguished moans of a small man pinned to the floor of the cab by a tall lady's stiletto heel.

The middle-aged man, still wearing his derby, continued to embrace his newfound love. They climbed out of the cab hand-in-hand and walked into the cocktail bar on the corner.

As passengers tumbled from the taxicab, an onlooker impersonated a television announcer's voice-- "There are one million stories in the Naked City...." He was quickly interrupted by a raspy voice from the rear that added, "and by tomorrow they'll be a helluva lot more!" The crowd cheered.

Ear-splitting sounds from taxi horns blared out in defiance of the logjam. The overcrowded taxicab finally emptied and moved slowly back into traffic. The two hanger-oners released their grip as the cab drove away.

It was time for me to get serious and swim north to my appointment on Central Park West.

\* \* \* \* \* \* \* \*

I allowed memories of previous job interviews to float in the currents of my mind. I seemed to have grown immune to the slashing hail. Perhaps my face was numb. How does one meet a chairman of the board wearing stone-like frozen features? I could neither smile nor chew gum. The weather was just as cruel in the high rent district as it is on 33rd Street.

I had seventeen job interviews in November and early December. At first I thought these men were blind to my potential. I felt qualified for the job openings. Later, l learned I may have failed for other reasons.

I met with key executives from advertising and publishing firms. They were cordial and accommodating –in fact overly so.

We climbed stairways both up and down in proper order as in elementary school where the smallest kid leads the others. I felt uncomfortable in front with interviewers' eyes upon me.

Dining room seating for lunch sometimes required an inordinate amount of time to allow the proper titles to be seated by rank. As a guest, I always sat next to Mr. Big. Everyone sat with back stiffened making it appear a robot was passing the broccoli.

I couldn't light a cigarette without an ashtray emerging seemingly from on high. Conversations touched on my family's social life in Englewood, N.J. where we lived at the time.

"When you lived in Engelwood was your family members of the Englewood Hunt Club?" That one line sent me downhill in a hurry. I told him a friend I played golf with, Ted MacAulliff, was reportedly carrying a gun the night he tried to murder his wife for undisclosed sins. . That said, was the sum and substance of my knowledge of guns.

"I'm not sure I even know where the Hunt Club is, gentlemen." I felt I was in the line of fire and wondered if the next question would query whether or not I played polo.

"Your kids go private schools?" I knew which Englewood school he was referring to.

"Yes, as a matter of fact they do. I have two girls who attend St. Cecilia's. I wouldn't have it any other way. The others are too young."

"How many kids do you have?"

"We have five."

Then someone tried to loosen the conversation and said something dumb like you must have been a busy man, or something as pointless as that.

"The house in Englewood was a big house – 100 years old, had high ceilings, needed lots of work. I was too busy buying lumber, tending the lawn, expanding the house, and general maintenance – all of that put membership in a club at the back of the bus.

The minute I said that, I wanted to pull it back and swallow it. But the black guy in the group didn't seem to mind.

"You guys, I'm sure, have been through that -- maybe you still do some heavy lifting so I'm sure you all understand.

"Yes, we sure do, said one."

Club membership could be a rite of passage to these guys and others I interviewed with. I imagined I carried he wrong passport.

A classic case occurred at Moloney, Reagan & Schmidt, a leading newspaper representative company. The years I spent at the Jersey Journal, selling retail advertising, I thought were worthy of at least a mention. The

Journal was one of M.R.S.'s's leading metropolitan dailies, but no. The subject wasn't even broached.

MRS dealt in national advertising—I sold retail advertising. I personally sold almost every major retail store in the county—from one of the largest women's shoe stores, retailing Balancinaga

High style shoes and Michael Carlin brands, plus several brands even Fifth Avenue had trouble ordering.

Are Sears, Safeway and National City Bank national enough? But I guess the stigma of retail put me in the back of the bus, one more time.

Judging from what I had seen so far, there wasn't a guy at the table who would last five minutes if they took him off his cushyAutomotive and P&G accounts and had him try to sell just one ad every Thursday to Moloney's Meat Market and have his ad fill the butcher shop with customers. If not, your ass was grass.

I interviewed with an advertising manager that was pleasant

But had nothing relevant to say. Next, two senior salesmen who didn't have much to say along the lines of the job responsibility interviewed me. I thought the MRS deal was dead until I got a call from one of the managers. He invited me to lunch. "

"We've been talking about you and I thought the sales staff

ought to get a look at you." I accepted, of course. I wanted to ask him, after he delivered the invite, "Why?" I had the same question at the conclusion of lunch the following week when six of their salesmen joined us. I wondered, "Do these guys do this every week? "

'Business' had not yet been mentioned. Lunch was finished. The luncheon check sat on the table waiting to be paid. I wondered if anyone was interested in hearing that I was named Salesman of the Year, twice at the Jersey Journal.

"Is that where the trophy winner holds it long enough for a photo and then puts it back in the storage room until same time next year?" one guy asked. Sarcasm dripped from every word.

"Which of you guys was salesman of the year for M.R.S last year,' I asked.

There was some stumbling and mumbling but no answer.

"I guess he was too busy to have lunch with us, and I can't blame him," I added, and then continued.

"No. There's no trophy award, or group photos at our newspaper. Just money. Hopefully, big fat checks, all over and above salary. We don't do trophies, or group photos and I don'trecall ever seeing a storage room."

That did it. The entire table suddenly turned quiet. I thanked everyone for lunch. Shook hands with each guy and said, "Hope you don't mind but I gotta catch a train." Mr. Big apologized.

"Us salesmen can handle rejection better than anyone else, can't we?" He smiled. "You handled yourself quite well, Marty. I just wish the decision was entirely up to me."

"Don't be silly. I wouldn't fit in anyway. You don't have a Salesman of the Year Award!" He laughed, and added, "Maybe it's time we did, Marty." He waved to me when I left.

*　　*　　*　　*　　*　　*　　*　　*

A cabbie leaned on his horn a little longer than usual. The blast brought me back from recalling my past. I continued trudging into the present. Ziff's apartment was on the corrner.

# Part 4
# I Meet Bill Ziff

The doorman acknowledged that Mr. Ziff was expecting me. A small voice on the intercom told him to send me up.

Mr. Ziff's Irish maid, who I perceived belonged to the small voice, offered to take my trench coat, my water-soaked hat and everything else that was wet, which was everything. I could strip naked and still be wet.

She asked me if I'd like to remove my boots and I was sorry later I didn't take the old gal up on her offer.

Mr. Ziff was waiting in the living room, flat on his back, treating the pain from a slipped disc. We greeted one another. He reached up, grabbed my hand and said, "Hi, Marty," with a strong handshake and a smile. I said "Hi, Mr. Ziff." He asked me to call him Bill.

"Would you like a cup of coffee? We'll have wine with lunch." I said yes to the coffee.

He raised himself slowly from a reclining position. I noticed that we were within an inch in height and guessed he weighed about fifteen pounds more than I did. We both had dark hair. He appeared to be about the same age as me. The similarities ended there.

He owned the Company -- sixteen magazines worth an estimated one billion dollars. I was looking for a job.

"What happened at Seeburg?" he asked. "They didn't respond to your letter."

It was like a bolt from the blue! Wow! I mean Wow!! Talk about getting to the point in a hurry! I hadn't even stopped dripping.

By way of explanation, I told him I had asked for letters of recommendation from some of my former employers: The Seeburg Corp., Cash Box, Billboard, and perhaps the Jersey Journal, I wasn't sure.

And so I g guessed the only one who failed to respond was Jack Gordon, President of Seeburg. Since he was also the one who fired me, I had a mark against me before I opened my mouth. A sticky wicket, as the Brits say. I tried to explain.

"The Seeburg Corporation went out of business on Dec. 5, 1965. I was let go that same day along with the other employees. They closed the plant.

"The officers of the company, as far as I knew, were the only ones retained for a short period. I have no explanation why Gordon did not send a letter of recommendation. Since the company went out of business, it seemed academic. It appeared to satisfy Bill. He said, "the others all wrote glowing letters of recommendation."

That made me feel good. Winning 3 to 1 was okay but I had the playoffs and the finals to win, yet.

When I was an ad agency account exec at a small agency we handled Seeburg. Gordon asked me to write some ad copy for Seeburg's new LP. I wrote six different lines charged him $500. He said he liked them all. He never paid the bill. I didn't see any point in relating stories like this to Bill Ziff. Aside from the obvious, he may have asked me why I later went to work for this guy.

"What made you leave Cash Box and join Seeburg?"

"I was earning $12,500 at Cash Box. Gordon offered me $20,000 and made me regional vice-president.

"My 'region' ran from Miami to Maine. I was seldom home. I arrived home one Sunday morning to change clothes. I had to attend an industry function in Virginia.

"All five of our kids came chasing through the house into the foyer. I thought they were coming to greet me. They made a left hand turn at the doorway and raced up the circular staircase without saying a word.

"As a result, Maureen and I discussed the plusses and minuses of my job the following week. She gave me an ultimatum. Choose her or the job. We decided I'd quit Seeburg no later than March 17, St. Patrick's Day. Seeburg beat me to the punch by three months."

Bill asked me about other job changes I made. "You worked for Seagram's, Stores Magazine, The Jersey Journal, Billboard, Cash Box, and then Seeburg. Correct?" I nodded. He was looking for a reason for the moves. I had no plan. I wound up practically telling him my life story.

"Why did you change jobs every two years?"

"Usually for money." I really hadn't thought of it before.

"You stayed two years or less at each job except Cash Box, where you were employed for seven years."

That observation brought total silence since I didn't really have an answer. So I told a story.

"I was an advertising clerk at Seagram's for four years. Some men occupied the same desk for a total career. I didn't want that.

"My desk was in my boss's office. He was Media Manager in charge of buying advertising in the nation's magazines and newspapers.

"Sales representatives called on him almost daily. I learned the difference between the salesman who wastes time asking my boss about his wife and kids and little else; and the salesman who sells the merits of his publication and relates them to Seagram sales."

"Why did you leave?"

"I wanted to be a sales rep."

"Did you call on Time or Newsweek or magazines that were established?"

"I don't remember filling out an application for the top magazines. They told me I didn't have enough experience. I remember talking to the New York Times. I still remember the gentleman's unusual name. It was Carroll J. Carroll.

"He spent time with me. He told me there was opportunity at the Times. He wanted me to start in the Classified Ad Department. I had a good telephone voice, he said. I imagined myself calling. on little old ladies trying to sell their broken sewing machine or cracked dishes or a threadbare blanket."

Mr. Carroll laughed. He said there was no such classification. I'd be selling Display/Classified, he said. "Corporations who wished to sell five or ten stories of heavy equipment," he continued, "that could be worth millions and require a half page or a full page ad worth thousands of dollars. That's a lot more than a threadbare blanket."

"Did the leading magazines still have training positions, then?" Bill asked.

"They may have. I thought I was a little old for that, Bill. I wasn't interested. I wanted to start selling at the top."

Tell me about Stores Magazine. First off, who is it, what is it, who publishes it?"

"I'll try to make it sound less strange than the operation was. That will be difficult. It's owned by the N.R.D.G.A., the Natl. Retail of Dry Goods Association. It was my first job after Seagram's. Maybe the worse move I ever made. Thank goodness I still lived at home.

During the course of my interview with H.O. Bell, the advertising director, something must have been said that I misconstrued; something that caused me to believe I'd be paid $100 per week .I started the following Monday. I learned that it was a straight commission job. There was no turning back, or at least I thought that the case.

The first ad I sold was to the Steinway Piano Company. Mr. John Steinway listened to my pitch and agreed to advertise. He signed a contract for one full page. When I told Mr. Bell about my accomplishment he fluffed off my victory. He said, "Yeah, sure. I expected that. That's why I sent you up there." I was crushed.

Stores Magazine sent me into the heart of the garment center where I met fascinating men while we waited to be called up by buyers. These men knew nothing about advertising. I knew nothing of velvet or satin. Or ruffles. They sold zippers, buttons, and piping that was sewed onto the collar and cuffs of little girl's dresses. "I sold 100,000 dresses to Little Miss Sunshine at the beginning of the season." I was impressed.

Another man told me he sold millions of dollars worth of zippers to men's jacket manufacturers. These men sold buttons some made buttonholes. They supplied cotton, wool, and linen depending on what was needed.

Everyone was Jewish except me. The garment center is comprised of companies that form an industry. As far as I could tell, the industry was totally Jewish.

The buyers called out the names of the vendors – "Abe Salesman", "Hymen Edelstein", "Mar Sundeck", and no one paid any attention. Then when my turn came, they'd hear, "Martin Toohey" and everyone would turn to look at the Gentile.

The buyers seldom bought anything from me but they treated me like a regular – nice guys. "We sell tons of merchandise to

Retailers like B Altman," the guys at S.Gloss and Co. told me." That's who should buy your ad." I got more help from those guys than I did from H.O. Bell and the other salesmen.

I asked Mr.. Bell to meet with me each afternoon to discuss sales even though I had little sales to discuss. That's when he told me the inside stories at Stores. There were the Buckley's, mother and son. She acted like the Queen of the May. He just tagged along. She bragged that they lived high up in the luxury apartments on Grammacy Park. "She told me one morning that her apartment was so luxurious that Fran Warren lived in the same building. Ms.Warren was a pop singer with the big bands.

Mr. Bell told me to stay away from Mrs. Buckley and her son. She once told me they had dinner on two consecutive nights at Luchows, a famous restaurant.

Mr. Bell told me that the first night she paid with a phony receipt or I.D. The second night the son paid with a phony receipt. Mr. Bell felt sorry for me. He'd start paying me $40 per week. Well! Was my mother glad to hear that."

I wanted to get to the Jersey Journal part of my life. It had a sensibility to it. Newspapers were common. The idea of calling on retailers for advertising made sense. It made sense compared with the strange jobs I was talking about Bill saw the merit in my selling display advertising for a family newspaper. Since the Jersey Journal was a long drive over the George Washington Bridge into Jersey City, I decided to quit college. I had cumed about two years of marketing and advertising credits while attending evenings. I had no awards to show for my school success but did allow a buddy to talk me into writing a column for the school newspaper. My daytime job at the Journal paid bonuses, each year if one made his budget and I did. One bonus helped me buy an engagement ring for my marriage to Maureen.

The Journal called for long hours. It was a long drive. The staff was disciplined. They worked their sales region in the morning when the stores opened, making calls until lunch and spending the afternoon I called on a variety of retailers-- designed and laid out retailer's ads, wrote the advertising copy, and delivered proofs for accuracy. It was truly a breeding ground where nice people tend to those who wanted to advance in advertising sales.

Each Monday morning, a short well-dressed man exited his limousine while his chauffeur waited. I asked the driver who this guy was. His name was S.I. Newhouse, owner of the Jersey Journal and one dozen other newspapers. He'd go on to become the largest publisher of magazines and newspapers in the country. I was hired by Billboard through a high school friend who worked there. The Billboard sales force left the office only to pee, seldom if ever to make a honest-to-goodness sales call.

After I made regular calls on Tenth Avenue, he hub of he industry; and Philadelphia's 30th Street Station, another hub, I told the ad manager that I'd like to start calling on the east coast -- from Miami to Maine. .

He told me his salesmen only made telephone calls once each year when the Annual Year-End Issue was published. I remember my boss asking me, "What are you going to say to distributors on the east coast? " I couldn't believe my ears. "I'll think of something," I said, in a cynical tone. I gained permission to open the east coast. The ad manager thought I was nuts, as did the two salesmen.

I began calling on very wholesaler from Miami to Maine. I forget the percent increase in ad linage but it was considerable.

Pay increase time came around approximately one year later. Everyone got the same increase. The guys who only left the office to pee and the guy, (namely me) who spent half the year in towns like Tecjmseh, SC; andVariarible, DE; and Intercourse, MI. fighting and almost wrestling for every scrap of advertising from the wholesalers.

I called Hilmer Stark, our manager in Chicago, to let him know of my bitter disappointment.

"Marty, I know how you must feel. We'll make it up to you next time. When are you and your lovely wife planning on having another baby," he asked.

"There's not going to be a next time, Hilmer. Once is enough. And my salary shouldn't have anything to do with my pay raises. "

Dick Ford called from Chicago. Dick was my immediate superior and one of my favorite people.

"Mart, give me a chance to make it up to you. Let's have you travel to New England on business each week, with the family, in the summer, as often as you desire and let us pick up the tab to have you stay over at your favorite resort – Cape Cod- all on the house. Take from Friday morning to Monday afternoon."

I couldn't believe my ears.

"Dick, I know you want what's best for me. But Hilmer stands im our way. "Thank you for coming to my aid Dick, but no thanks"

I called Perry Wachtel wino owned DePerri Advertising Agency.

"Perry, this is Marty Toohey. I understand your looking for a new account executive. Can we talk?

I stayed with Perry for two years. He had just won a major super market account. Dilbert's was a large east coast food chain, smaller than the A&P, larger than Best Foods.

Wednesday afternoon the entire ad agency helped me re-enact the equivalent of World War II. I played the General and commanded the troops. We "invaded" seven daily New York newspapers with our ad copy delivered by deadlines set between 4 and 5 pm.

Perry played golf on Wednesdays. That's one of the reasons he hired me.

*　　*　　*　　*　　*　　*　　*　　*

The snow was still falling in Central Park. It was deep in every direction with shaped mounds from the wind. The sun had set to shine in faraway places around the world. But Central Park was black and totally devoid of life.

Bill observed that we had been talking; at least I had been talking, for most of the afternoon, some four or more hours. "You explained more than a dozen predicaments, situations that you found yourself in. In the telling, your description went out into right field, turned left through some magic you seem to have, then veered left again and came back to the plate scoring a home run. You returned to complete your point every time," he concluded.

"And so we have a dilemma." We had been standing and now we both decided to sit down.

"On the one hand, you have totally mismanaged your career. You left several positions before you had a chance to reap any benefit; or you took the wrong job for the wrong reasons. We\ discussed that earlier. Either way, you were destined to crash.

"You should be meeting now with Mr. Fleischman, owner of

The New Yorker, on your way to being named publisher of his magazine." Bill allowed a long pause to elapse before he continued. I was almost shattered. I felt like a total failure.

I couldn't believe he thought me capable of being publisher of anything, let alone one of the most prestigious magazines in the business. Not after that verbal resume!

"Instead, you're sitting here looking for a job."

I felt as though I had been slapped down face first, on a cold marble floor. That was the knockout blow. I wanted to leave. He continued.

"We've made the same mistake, over and over -- not hiring the applicant because there's no opening," he said. "When we later contact that individual, he's already been hired by someone else." He stopped for a moment before he continued.

"I don't want to lose you," he said. "I think we should stand you in a corner until we have an opening."

I didn't want to get ahead of myself but I thought I had just been hired. Standing in an inside corner was better than standing outside looking in.

"You met Ms. Eddy," he said. "She helped you earlier today." "Call her. She'll make an appointment for you with David E. Davis, Jr. He's publisher of Car and Driver."

I left his apartment. The same doorman was on duty. We smiled at each other.

"Looks like it's beginning to end," he said, motioning to the weather outside.

I didn't want to disagree but I felt the day was just beginning. Even the carolers outside Bloomingdale's were singing in tune.

# Meet DED. Jr.

## Puligny-Montrachet?

The next day I received a phone call from Anita Eddy who laughingly asked if I was still wet. I asked her if the tide had finally gone out in her reception room. . We laughed together.

Mr. Ziff wanted me to call David E. Davis, Jr., publisher of Car and Driver Magazine, after taking the company's psychological sales aptitude test.

"Don't be concerned, Mr. Toohey. No one thinks you're weird." She laughed again. "It's been mandatory for all sales applicants for about five years."

"Anybody ever fail?" I asked.

"We have too many weirdos working here for me to notice!" Anita Eddy was not your typical executive secretary. I was getting to like her more and more.

I called the psychological testing company and got an appointment for that week. The following day I read twelve back issues of Car and Driver at the library from cover to cover. I compared it with its competition and Car and Driver won hands down. All the other car magazines were your typical greasy fingernail zoom-zoom-buff books. Car and Driver was slick and sophisticated both editorially and graphically. I paid special attention to Davis' monthly column. It told me a lot about him. The middle initial and the "Jr." sounded a bit pompous. The caricature which accompanied his columns enhanced the pomposity. Handlebar mustache, arrogant over-the-shoulder look, and his personal writing style told me he worked at celebrity.

I learned that David E. Davis, Jr. was a star in the automotive enthusiast universe, but a star nonetheless. I called him later that day and assumed that Ziff had provided him with the preliminaries. He had.

"David E. Davis, Jr. this is Martin Thomas Toohey." It occurred to me that adding a "Jr." to my name would have given my straightforward introduction a nice ring. I resisted.

"Martin Thomas I have been awaiting your call." So far so good. I thought it wise to establish myself as a reader of his magazine and especially his column.

"I too find myself 'lost in the latitudes', as you write in your current column criticizing today's automotive design. But my personal fate is far more grievous, at least to me. I am in search of gainful employment as I explained to Mr. Ziff. I'd like to join Car and Driver's sales staff."

"Mr. Ziff told me about his meeting with you. I would like very much to meet the individual our Chairman found reason to spend an entire afternoon with. I have trouble getting in to see Ziff even when he calls me to his office to scold me. Are you available for lunch Monday at Argenteiul? Say, twelve noon?"

I told him I was, provided he told me how to spell it. I think he thought I was kidding. He gave me the cross street on Third Avenue.

So here we go, I thought. The David E. Davis, Jr. tour is about to begin. The handlebar mustache and arrogant over-the-shoulder look would meet me at lunch rather than in his office. I was about to meet the man behind the most sophisticated car magazine to ever sell off a newsstand. I felt slightly intimidated.

\* \* \* \* \* \* \* \*

The maitre d' led me to a reserved table and I positioned myself so I could see Davis enter the reception area. The restaurant was quite busy. I felt that our table was a select one. I ordered coffee. He arrived about ten minutes later and there was no question that this was the man.

Davis cut quite a swath  as he removed his muted glen plaid cape. His cap matched the cape.  The maitre'd obviously knew him and led him to our table. Davis wasn't quite six feet tall but looked taller. He wore a woolen suit of European cut  and approached me with long confident steps.

"Martin Thomas Toohey, I presume."

"Mr. Davis, sir." I stood. We shook hands.

"We seem to have an unusually large luncheon crowd here today. The Pan-American Games must be in town." I assumed he was being facetious. He was.

"Would you care to exchange your  cup of homespun coffee for a glass of Puligny Montrachet? It will make our initial introduction more cordial."

I agreed.

"I don't mean to put down Senor Juan Carioni, the gentleman who owns this joint, but most find his coffee vile."

"As I do," I said. "There is nothing mild about this coffee. I still remember the fragrance of my mother's coffee.  My wife comes in a close second. I pay almost no attention to coffee served in restaurants. I just sip it until I can dismiss it. Which makes your offer of Puligny Montrachet sound inviting."  I thought I was holding my own, conversationally.

As with Ziff's height, weight and age that's about all Davis and I had in common  as far as appearances went. My conservative Brooks Brothers suit was the antithesis of his flowing garb. I estimated that a tailor could cut twice the number of garments for me from the material required for one David E. Davis, Jr. double-breasted suit , cape, coat and vest.

He had auburn hair, longer than average but well coifed. The handle bar mustache and beard blended well. Davis could play Mark Twain or a southern politician or David E. Davis, Jr., a role he probably created. I wore a crew cut in those days, fashionable in the sixties, unless you were protesting the war, smoking pot and listening to Janis Joplin records. Having read a backlog of Davis' columns I doubted he was a Sinatra fan.

Davis had a cherub-like look to his face and a vague scar that crossed the far end of his left eyelid which in no way detracted from his classical features. He worked at Road & Track magazine in southern California before joining Ziff-Davis. The commonality of same name was a coincidence. Ziff wanted Davis to take Sports Cars Illustrated, a look-alike race car magazine, and turn it into something else.

The "something else" turned out to be a magazine called Car and Driver. Both Ziff and the world of automotive enthusiasts were elated. The publication soon enjoyed vast circulation and advertising growth and Davis became an icon.

"I was a southern California race car driver who had a cushy job writing for Road & Track during the week while racing a car on weekends. The world was my oyster, or "erster" as they might say in The Bronx -- until I went upside down."

I took note of the erster in The Bronx comment but figured I'd let it go. "I take it your going 'upside down' means you finished the race on your face."

"On my nose for part of the way until it came off. An alert spectator spotted it laying on the racetrack and handed it to one of the medics. They stuck it back on in surgery. During the first post-op months I kept wondering if it would fall off or perhaps wind up in my handkerchief after a vigorous sneeze."

Judging from the dates he referred to I figured this all happened about three or four years ago. He's still retelling the story and having a good time relating it. I told him the patch job added to his stature whereas a wooden nose would simply serve as a distraction. He laughed.

"I wonder if Ziff would have hired me anyway."

"I doubt that something as trivial as an artificial nose would prevent Mr. Ziff from allowing you to invent another winner for his stable."

"I got Ziff's phone call six months to the day I crashed," said Davis. "I could no longer race and I didn't want to stay at Road & Track as just another editorial grunt."

"Ziff's offer to allow me to invent a winner, as you aptly put it, was an offer too good to turn down. My wife Norma and I were living like southern California celebrities with no money. It didn't matter. I was a well known race car driver and Road & Track is the car buff's bible out there. Lower California was my erster.

"The problem was that New York is not California. But as Norma aptly put it, 'And California ain't New York, Mr. Publisher'. That did it."

Just as I began to wonder who was interviewing whom, Davis turned the conversational tide.

"So you're an Irish Catholic ad guy from The Bronx."

"Is that how Ziff billed me?"

"Au contraire, Martin Thomas. You received rave reviews from Mr. Ziff. My observations are based on our prior telephone conversations. You'll recall you spoke of Cardinal Hayes High School and your early days in The Bronx."

I thought it interesting that Davis commented on my background rather than my  sales experience. I wondered if he'd been influenced by Ziff.

"If truth be told I may be the only  Irish Catholic advertising guy from The Bronx that I know of," I said. "Two of the guys from our neighborhood went to prison.  Others stayed in The Bronx and became cops and firemen. A  few of us got degrees on the G.I. Bill. No one I know of went into advertising. Maybe  Ziff never did either, until I came along."

"You did everything right, Martin Thomas."

Davis made several choices for lunch. He ordered Vitel Tonee, which I learned was a cold veal dish, sliced and served with potato salad. I ordered Tallarines (Tal-A-Reenis), a linguini dish served in casserole with beef and tomato sauce for two reasons. I could pronounce it, and it was as close as I was going to get to spaghetti ragu. Davis ordered a bottle of red wine.

"Malbec is an Argentine wine much like a cabernet," said Davis. "Senor Carioni reserves his Malbec Mendoza for special guests. It will taste wonderful with our beef and veal."

The restaurant had filled to capacity. Foreign inflections flowed from tables like waters from international shores. I may have been the only clean shaven face in the place. A couple of weeks ago I dined on the usual corned beef sandwich with a juke box wholesaler in the back room of his cluttered office. I was enjoying the lofty transition if even for the moment. Davis resumed where our conversation left off before we ordered lunch.

"The absence of Irish Catholics and Jews in advertising was a phenomenon until recently," said Davis. "The ad biz was practically founded by White Anglo Saxon Protestants, of which I am a reluctant member. WASPS controlled the ad agencies." I thought of the General and my seventeen interviews with the Ivy league set.

"The partnership of Doyle, Dane Bernbach and Volkswagen, an incongruity if ever there was one, changed the face of the advertising business. A Jewish advertising agency now managed a German car account. Talk about cultural breakthroughs."

I felt that I was experiencing my own cultural breakthroughs these past few days. Lunching one day with a young multi-millionaire chairman of the board who's marketing vision astounded me. Today, dining with a former race car driver whose tastes run International when it comes to fashion, food, cars and wine. I began to feel quite ordinary in my Brooks Brothers attire and crew cut.

"The import car business is led by Dutchmen and Dagos, Swedes and Brits and of late, the Japanese," said Davis. "With the exception of the Japanese, their U. S. headquarters are located here on Park Avenue and close by in New Jersey. This is quite convenient since each has a gentleman at the top who is as important to us as the Chairman of GM, Ford or Chrysler. Although we love 'em all, of course."

Since you'll be working with these half-breeds you should read "Beyond the Melting Pot" unless you already have. Milton Glaser and Daniel Patrick Moynihan, a lad from your clan in the Bronx, no less, wrote it. The authors agree that assimilation of nationalities – Dagos, Swedes, Blacks, whomever - in truth, does not take place. You'll find the book comforting as you speak to the Italians from Fiat and the Germans from Mercedes-Benz and so forth. Pick it up.

While we're on the subject of books, one Marshall McLuhan, who prides himself a Psychologist, has recently shaken up the "ad biz" with his pronouncements on what we're all really doing —studies in what makes certain people by certain products. McLuhan says, "The Medium Is the Message". Don't disagree right away. Pick that up too. If nothing else you'll have interesting reading material while you cool your heels in the ad agency reception rooms around town.

Davis exhibited a business and social lifestyle I was unfamiliar with. I owned and drove only cars made in Detroit. The executive levels he made reference to towered above the lowly elevator floors of my previous sales responsibilities.

I thought of my experience with small Jersey City retail advertisers who struggled to pay the rent and their advertising bills. Moloney's Meat Market, Ross Jewelers and Wenton's Shoe Store -- a butcher, a jeweler and a shoe store owner. Davis is talking about business associations with the top executives at Mercedes-Benz, Jaguar, Volkswagen-- industry leaders, worldwide. The closest I ever got to the automotive business was selling ads to used car dealers.

My Billboard and Cash Box client list in New York City wasn't much more impressive. It included wholesalers on Tenth Avenue who sold juke boxes and pinball machines from street level store fronts. Granted, their business was lucrative and their lifestyle affluent, they were truly from the other side of the tracks. More to the point, Tenth Avenue was from the other side of the ocean. Davis continued to explain the import car business.

"You will be dealing with a League of Nations. It's called the Import Car Industry. It is a major source of Car and Driver's revenue."

I almost gagged on my spaghetti ragu. If Davis said what I thought he said, I was just hired. I took a sip of wine, swallowed hard and allowed him to continue.

"There's a book just published that you should read. It was co-written by Nathan Glaser and one of your very own, Daniel Patrick Moynihan, Irish Catholic congressman from The Bronx. Which gets us back to what we were talking about before the waiter interrupted.

"'Beyond the Melting Pot' interprets the cultural differences between nationalities after they arrive in America. Italians and Germans and Swedes and that league of nations you'll be calling clients starting Monday.

Moynihan's book was practically written for this auspicious occasion."

I made two mental notes -- the titles of the two books and the starting date of my new job, and not necessarily in tthat order.

# I Meet C/D Editorial

## On a bongo board

No provision had been made for my arrival at Ziff-Davis. I didn't expect a sixth floor welcoming committee, just a desk.

The Car and Driver sales offices were either camouflaged or had moved to Dallas. I was sent to the tenth floor. It resembled the sixth. I wondered if I had been hired in the first place. Perhaps it was all hallucination. Employees walked hurriedly through the halls. No one looked at me. I could have been in search of the Empire State Building.

"Is Car and Driver on this floor?" I asked.

"I think they're on the other side."

I felt like asking, "The other side of what, your holiness?

'Are the Car and Driver sales offices on this floor?"

"I'm with Pop Photo."

"Congratulations. Are the Car and Driver sales offices on this floor?"

"Davis's office is down the hall. He should know." I would think so. Davis was conducting a rather informal editorial meeting. I was invited in. He sat behind his cigar which sat behind his mouth which sat directly beneath an eight cylinder chrome plated a Mercedes Benz engine attached to the ceiling.

Several editorial types were slouched in chairs. Everyone was smoking which suited me just fine. Nothing like a cigarette when you don't know what to do with your hands. Two ash trays perched atop Davis' engine for those out of reach of his desk. Other seemingly lesser staffers blended against the four walls. I tried to join them.

I recognized star columnist Brock Yates who glided back and forth on a bongo board. Davis gave me a broad introduction that may have included my name. Yates said, "Hi" and continued balancing himself from side to side on his board. Some of the others nodded in my direction.

An attractive young lady with a Canadian accent addressed Davis in soft spoken four-letter words. She was making her pitch to interview a famous race car driver in Texas. Her name was Chris McCall. She was associate editor. She was also the only female in the room.

"A story on the reclusive if not virtually invisible Jim Hall would knock our readers' collective asses off. No one has met him, Dave."

I learned that Jim Hall, a race car driver, had designed and then built his own race car named Chaparral after the Texas bird. The car's design was unusual to say the least—kind of a horizontal black version of Casper the Ghost. Front cover photographs of the car appeared in every car magazine and later in the newsweeklies. Afer he won each race, and he won every race he entered, Hall would drive his jet black racer into the Chaparral garage and send an emissary to pick up his trophy. No photographs of the engine had ever appeared anywhere.

"Dave, the son-of-bitch is a mystery. Jim Hall gets more publicity by hiding than if he went on public tour for chrissakes! I can get him to talk." McCall stamped out a cigarette in one of the ashtrays on Davis's desk and quickly lit up another. She appeared to be playing a Hollywood role but she managed it well.

"And how often do you think you'll have to roll over for this ghost before he allows you to unsnap his hood?" asked Davis. McCall deliberately fell backwards onto the lap of a seated staffer, allowed her skirt to climb up her thighs, and said, "If you think I'm going to fly to some Godforsaken sand pit in Texas just so I can shake my ass for this weirdo race driver, you haven't been listening."

"What makes you think he'll see you?" "I just spoke with him. He said he could have lunch with me tomorrow."

" You didn't say that. Why are you wasting our time? Go!"

McCall stood up, stamped out her cigarette and swiveled her hips toward the office door. "It's the way I get my jollies, Davie boy. I'll call you as soon as I unsnap his hood."

The staffers filed out as the meeting broke up. Davis asked me to stay. He called out to Yates. "Brock, get your Goddamn bongo board outta here before I take a header. I've got to fly to Frankfurt tonight and I don't want to get off the airplane looking like a returning war veteran." Davis asked me to close his office door.

"Well, at least you got to see how the natives in the zoo perform. And as you may have discerned, the zookeeper is not always in charge."

I commented on Chris McCall's performance. "She has a great editorial mind. Sees the big picture but can spot fly shit on a leopard.  Been here about a year. She's married to John Jerome, editor of our very own Stereo Review, located here on the eighth floor. Her brother Bruce is already making a name for himself as a writer. He's also an accomplished artist and a very funny guy. They're an editorial family.

"Since we are a car magazine I wouldn't want this to get out but the great Chris McCall has never driven a car," said Davis. After observing the eccentricities of the editorial staff I wouldn't be surprised if they couldn't read or write. Nonetheless, they sure managed to turn out one hell of a monthly magazine. I asked Davis where the sales offices were 1located. I was surprised when he led me to them.

"Follow me." We walked down the hall together and stopped inside the art department.

"Gene Butter meet Marty Toohey, the latest addition to our sales staff." The art director was sitting in an antique barber chair. He held a magnifying glass in one hand, a tired cigar in the other. A small photograph sat under the glass. He barely looked up to acknowledge the introduction by waving to me with his cigar.

"Is he Larry's replacement?" asked Butter.

The question stunned me. I wondered if he referred to Larry Leins, the sales manager of the magazine, who never interviewed me, yet his name appeared on the masthead. Davis responded indirectly to Butera's question and artfully changed the subject.

"The die has not yet been cast, Butera. Uncertainty hangs in the air not unlike your questionable graphics as we approach deadline each month."

Gene smiled, released the side handle on his barber chair and laid back as though he were about to receive a shave. "Here it comes," said Butera. "The saga of the potted plant." He stuck the cigar in his mouth and closed his eyes. Davis turned to me.

"The only constant in Mr. Butera's work style is that nasty little dago cigar he keeps clenched between his teeth. We never know whether his camera lens will allow us to see what the featured car in question looks like until the magazine is printed. Of course by then it's too late to make changes. Mr. Butera has a habit of photographing cars deliberately positioned behind towering potted plants for art's sake." The art director laughed out loud at Davis's criticism of his work.

"The story never changes, said Butera who looked at me. "I once photographed a classic BMW behind a potted plant. The shot called for it. And he's still chastising me!"They we having a good time. So was I.

"Yes, unfortunately BMW President Max Hoffman didn't feel that way. I felt we were about to start World War lll when he called," said Davis.

Butera asked if I had met "Herr Hoffman" as yet. I laughed.

"I haven't even met my office yet!"

"Mr. Toohey will meet 'Herr Hoffman' in due time, said Davis. " Meanwhile, promise me you'll stay out of greenhouses. The name of our magazine is Car and Driver, not Flower and Garden. " Davis led me back to the main corridor.

"Dave, was Gene referring to Larry Leins?" I asked. "I wondered why I haven't met him."

"I had to fire him two weeks ago," replied Davis. "I guess you'll never meet him. We were entertaining a small group of clients at the Bahamas

Road Races in Nassau and Mr. Liens had too much to drink," said Davis. "Larry's face fell into a plate of mashed potatoes. Everyone at our table tried to make polite small talk but Larry was hard to ignore. He kept clawing at the linen tablecloth in survival fashion. Better he had quietly slipped away.

"I saw no reason to call you. It's probably all for the better, at least from your point of view. Have you ever managed a sales staff?"

# I Meet Circulation

## Isn't that Satchmo playing?

Larry Sporn, VP Circulation, played from a different instrument than the rest of us..

His office windows were cloaked in black drapes. There was a tiny peep light on Larry's desk that illuminated his face, unfortunately. His stereo speakers blared at full fever pitch during one on one meetings in his office.

I had my first and last meeting with Larry the day I met him. Jack Teegarden was singing, "Do You Know What It Means To Miss New Orleans?" I tried to register disagreement over the direct mail cardsLarry used to promote C/D subscriptions. Business reply cards were inserted into the newsstand copies of the magazine. I tried to disagree with his methods. I wasn't sure he heard me over the music. I'm not sure I heard myself.

Each subscription card featured a photograph of a racecar with promotional copy that asked the reader to subscribe to C/D.

"Larry, you're using photographs of race cars that are forty years old. Makes us look like idiots." I had to shout over a different Louis Armstrong recording that he began to play.

Larry spun in his chair to a file cabinet, reached for a folder marked "subscription cards" or something similar, spun back in my direction and responded.

"The card you refer to generated a 28% return - - the highest return of any card we've ever used in your magazine. We'll continue to use it every month until the well runs dry. So forget about the age of the race- cars. Apparently your readers don't even know the difference. What's next?" I could barely hear him over Satchmo's solo on "Sleepy Time Down South".

"Larry, why does Motor Trend constantly get better newsstand display than Car and Driver? No matter what city I'm in Motor Trend is front and center on airport newsstands? Car and Driver is invisible. Motor Trend publishes three or four magazines. Ziff publishes sixteen!" Larry lit something before he spoke. It may have been a cigarette.

"Sometimes sixteen can be a problem. Especially in your case. Don't put your little car magazine on the same level as the big boys. Take Modern Bride for instance. They sell one million copies off the newsstands every month! Do you know how many women get married every month? I'll tell you how many women get married every month. Four million!

I said four million! Does Detroit sell four million cars every month? On your ass!" He was shouting above Satchmo's rendition of "Muskrat Ramble" which I once liked.

"Do you know what your ratio of sales is on newsstands?" he asked. "Runs only ten percent."

"How would I know? I don't receive copies of anything from you. "

"When did you ever ask?" he shouted. After this I thought I'd never ask.

"Modern Bride does a fifty-percent off the newsstand. That means they sell one million copies each month at $3.95 per copy and that makes Car and Driver look like it's not even worth unloading from the truck!"

I had other complaints but saw no point in pursuing them. Larry was going to do it his way. Period.

I happened to know that he had the full backing of Bill Ziff.

Larry and I shook hands. I closed the door behind me and squinted through the glare of sunlight in the outer offices.

Clerks looked up from their desks at another Interloper leaving -- one who dared enter the boss' sanctum sanctorum with a complaint.

Satchmo was playing, "Saint James Infirmary". I thought it appropriate.

# Special Interests
# * Special People

## Airplanes, Sports Cars, Motorcycles and Sailboats

Bill Ziff told me the editorial content of a magazine serves as a screen and attracts readers genuinely interested in the magazine's subject matter. It quickly came to my attention that most of the work force at Ziff Davis was there for the same reason.

Until I joined Ziff Davis I thought that anyone who rode motorcycles was a little off center. Nonetheless, Chris Farrell, a high school buddy and I rode to Harlem on his Harley to hear Billie Holiday sing "Lover Man". I guess Ziff-Davis changed me. I rode on the back of Farrell's motorcycle. It still sounded good playing on a worn out juke turntable. One couldn't hear "Lover Man" anywhere else in the Bronx. Besides, it gave us an excuse to ride the sickle.

One evening just after we landed at Le Mudder and dropped another ten nickels Into the jukebox, a policeman entered. He walked toward Christy and me. Since it was an all-black bar we assumed he was arresting one of the regulars. He wasn't.

"I want you two guys to saddle up and ride your horse back to the Bronx the same way you came in. They don't want you here, you don't belong here, and I'm certain you both are bright enough to never return."

Later, I had other opportunities to ride. I stretched a weeklong business trip to include a Los Angeles weekend. Some bike and car magazine guys

I compete with during business hours every week invited me to go dirt biking. They were Motor Trend and Cycle World guys. They assumed this Car and Driver guy from back east lived the same way they do. Play on weekends, play on weekdays, play whenever the sun is out and it almost never sets out there. Hell, I was just another enthusiast with a car magazine.

There were ten guys and two wives, all of whom were about 30 years old. I was 50. They all wore "Sons of Thunder" tee shirts with lightning bolts on the back. I had to re-wear a button-down Brooks Bros. dress shirt I made sales calls in the Friday before. Given the choice to bike ride or stop for rolls and buns after mass was a no-brainer. This was home for the weekend.

My sojourn began Sunday morning. I managed my Harley 100 yards to the top of a hill, clearly the entrance to L.A. 98. I felt like I was about to make my first sky dive. I was later informed that Rt. 98 was the most treacherous freeway in L.A. Motorists drive 150 to 200 mph on Sundays to "get even" for having to drive between 2 and 3 mph to work all week long.

It took me almost an hour to finally find an opening to enter L.A 98 as flocks of unleashed cars flew by apparently with no intention of ever stopping. I estimated it would take me two seconds throw the bike into high gear without getting hit in the doofus. I had the very next car pegged to arrive in 5 seconds.

One guy's poison is another guy's passion. Suddenly sixteen cars crashed and made a telescoped pile-up of wreckage. It left a small path to maneuver onto the freeway before all hell broke lose again. I kept it into high gear planning never to stop with that crowd behind me and barely made it to the off-ramp.

I found the dirt bikers riding, sliding and flying. There were the expected sighs of relief from my guys. Some said they ride Rt. 98 every Sunday, "for the fun of it".

Two biker friends tore to the bottom of the downhill dirt slope, launched as if they had rockets on board, and flew through the air to somewhere. "There goes Charlie and Rob," said one. "Let's go, we're next!" he shouted, to no one in particular. They were doing what they like to do. I found a mound and tempered it a while. Gave me time to choose between church and dirt biking.

I could almost smell the rolls and buns.

I saw pilots as aviators who walked through airline terminals carrying a large black briefcase which could have been a large lunch-- or appeared in war movies chasing an enemy who painted his airplane wings with red meatballs

I met our Ziff-Davis company pilot, Todd Wheeler, when he offered to fly my wife and me, me with two of our kids, to summer camp. My understanding was altered the moment we stepped on board.

I practically got a private flying lesson from Todd, the kids stayed glued to the windows sounding like tour guides. Maureen didn't want to land.

Todd waited for us to check the kids in and get back to his single wing beauty. The Piper took off, passed over Massachusetts, and dropped down at LaGuardia. Like the man says, "It's the only way to fly."

True to form, the next time we met Todd for a quick lift to the Bahamas he pulled up in his Porsche. True to form, another enthusiast. I never wanted to look at commercial ship again and decided to ask Mr. Ziff if I could use the Piper for my business trips. His response is not fitting for a family magazine such as this.

My knowledge of boats consisted of renting a putt-putt outboard tacked onto the stern of a rented rowboat in City Island where we swam.

Syd Rogers was publisher of Boating Magazine at the time. Syd raced ocean-going boats in trans-Atlantic crossings. Prior to that he played football for Army while a cadet at West Point.

The closest I ever got to a West Point cadet was at Yankee Stadium each year when Army played Navy and we stood outside and watched the cadets march in. That same Syd Rogers helped me buy my first sailboat-- a used fourteen foot Falcon. The price was a miniscule fraction of less than one percent of the cost of the boats Sid sailed. It made no difference to him.

I can still see Sid crawling down under the forecastle on his hands and knees wearing those gray flannel Brooks Bros. trousers and that navy blue blazer he seemed to live in.

He had the owner of the boat haul out the sails from stowage and spread them across the front lawn of the yacht club. He looked for pinpoint signs of wear and tear. "Pinholes can cost you the difference between first and second place in a race," he said.

When I told Sid I had no intention of racing my sailboat, he simply said, "Why not? You gonna piddle around the Sound all day?" That's all it took. I joined the Greenwich Racing Association and raced every week thereafter.

That was Syd. Solid gold. True blue. Lay down his life. Can you imagine racing in the America's Cup with Syd Rogers? Now that would be something to write about.

I'd be as impressed as anyone whenever a Jaguar passed. Until it passed. It can also be said of an MG or even a Porsche. These cars came from another world-- certainly not the world in which I lived. I soon found myself actually driving such cars on loan from the manufacturers and the Car and Driver test car pool -- cars that were in the process of being road tested by the editorial staff. Cars that the outside world didn't know about until car magazines put them on the front cover. I became an enthusiast!

I didn't shun the Shelby Mustangs, Pontiac Firebirds, Chrysler hemis or AMC Javelins. I was lucky to drive them, too. I guess I preferred the imports and still do.

I drove every two-seater and small import sedan during the 1970's. When I accrued enough to pay for one; the BMW Bavaria got the nod. Then the Fiat 1300 2-seater (for 5 kids) sports car, Alfa Romeos, Porsches, Jags, MG's, And so it went.

The only cameras I could identify were a "Brownie" which I heard about as a kid and the Kodak Instamatic -- yesterday's version of "A Camera for Dummies". Now I had a photo expert on my side of the counter—in fact, across the hall stationed behind a desk in the offices o f Popular Photography. The editor of Pop Photo, no less. I'd ask the age-old question, "Which camera should I buy?" The answers from seasoned photogs comprised an instant mini-course in photography. And the words Brownie or Instamatic were never mentioned again.

Up until the time I signed on with Car and Driver I poured out of subways and elevators and office buildings with the great unwashed, majorities just like me.

The men and women I lunched with and sat in on meetings with had names that were synonymous with accomplishment. Official statistics established major accomplishments by many of these individuals. Their record-breaking heroics took place in the air, on land and on water. Editors and staffers of Cycle Magazine, namely Gordon Jennings and Cooke Nielsen, were listed alongside their official speed records set on the salt flats in Utah. Buddy and golf partner Skeets Coleman broke the altitude record as an Air Force test pilot during WW II.

Jack Brown had been publisher of a number of Ziff Davis magazines before he became president of a division. Probably the best salesman I ever met. He told me he "rode the rails" -- he was talking freight trains-- in his teenage years. He wanted to emulate Jack London. Seemed he had traveled everywhere.

Jack was another born sailor. You just had to love him. He was a big cubby bear of a guy with a very deep voice that had a gravel tone to it from all the whiskey he drank. He didn't talk much about the book he was writing until it was published. "Incident on 125th Street" must have been published some time in the late 1960's. Based on a true murder story, a television network bought it for $20,000, according to Jack. He walked into my office one day and placed a personally signed copy on my desk without saying a word. .

I still talk to Joe Mesics. He owns a vineyard in the Napa Valley. For all I know he's as successful as the Gallo brothers. He'd never tell. We write each other regularly. He was publisher of Electronics Magazine when I met him. Incongruous though it may seem, I knew that when the computer came along he'd never buy one even though his business life abounded in things electronic. Joe was and still is a contrary s.o.b. No e-mail for him. He still types his letters on an old Royal workhorse each page sprinkled with typos as if it had measles. I complain that I cannot read them, to no avail.

Joe played football at Dartmouth but seldom spoke about his achievements on the field or anywhere else for that matter. He took great pleasure in putting down colleagues at Ziff Davis who boasted degrees from Yale and Harvard in subtle albeit noticeable ways. Joe was a Marine fighter pilot during the Viet Nam War and got his start at Ziff Davis working on Flying Magazine. He flies his own plane to this day.

I haven't written a title for this book, as yet. Up to this point, something like, "What A Wonderful Life" wouldn't be a bad title. We'll just have to wait until the right thing comes along.

But it couldn't have been better.

# CAR AND DRIVER GOES TO THE MOVIES

## Blessed are they who squirm

Advertising is sold in as many different ways as there are definitions of the word itself. What turns one buyer on doesn't necessarily work with another. Six different advertisers will buy advertising space in the same magazine for six different reasons. The advertising director of a small oil company once said to me that "clearly half of all the advertising that appears works. We just don't know which half! I guess our jobs are safe until they find the answer. "

Did the Baja 500 promotional parties help sell more ad pages in our magazine? Can't really say. Was it the slick marketing presentation we did for "Speed" Oldfield, top advertising honcho at AC Delco, that got us the business? Seemed to me that "Speed" was more accessible after the first Baja 500 party than before.

Time-Life Publishing flies clients in company jets to Washington D.C. presidential press conferences. That's entertaining on a "sky's the limit" budget. The meek and humble try to build relationships over guacamole and tequila in a godforsaken desert.

During the late sixties our Detroit manager thought he'd build a few relationships by showing John Frankenheimer's new racecar film, "Grand Prix", a natural tie-in for our magazine. We rented a downtown theater for a Monday night. RSVP's indicated a weak response. Our staff could wind up holding hands with each other in an empty theater. Who'd eat all the chili and beer during our afterglow party at the Ponchartrain?

David E. Davis, Jr. stood tall in the lobby of the theater like the great Poobah he was. We hoped enough of the "right" people would turn out to shake his hand. Media events are sometimes papered with lower ranked juniors looking for a freebee. Either that or a Vice-President decided to pass on the invite and send one of the kids. There are times when disappointment can be defeating.

Sales and editorial staffers stood around the theater lobby waiting to greet our guests if only they'd arrive. An air of failure filled the lobby. Terrible thoughts enter one's head at moments like these. Some take the dismissal personally. Others view it as a less than high regard for the magazine. Either way it's a form of rejection. Thin-skinned people need not apply.

Just before seven o'clock, when the film was supposed to start, cars began to swarm curbside forming lines at the theater's entrance. Wives and guests were dropped off. Other cars quickly replaced them. Hoards of familiar advertising and marketing faces could be seen walking toward us from the parking lot. Surprise after surprise arrived. No one paid much attention to our RSVP request. "We didn't think you'd run out of theater seats!" Ha-ha. "Who needs to RSVP for a movie?" Ha-ha. "Now if the invite included dinner at the Chop House!" Ha-ha. "Where do we go for the chili blast?" Ha-ha.

As for the quality of attendees, we even had a limo or two pull up, much like they do on Oscar night. Suffice to say that Ed Cole, president of General Motors, accompanied by his popular wife Dolly, strolled through the lobby in formal dress which surprised us. Cole approached our Poobah and shook his hand. Someone must have given Cole a ticket unless our promotion manager added his name to our mailing list in a moment of optimistic insanity.

"I told Dolly, 'You're always making me see movies that you like. Tonight we're going to a movie that I like'," said Cole laughing. "Thanks so much for having us, Dave. We're going to a charity ball after your movie. Your timing was perfect." That made Davis' night. Our jobs were safe.

As the lobby finally cleared a second limo drove up. The chauffeur opened the door and the tip of a long cigar emerged followed by a tall man in formal dress. Our Poobah turned to greet him.

"Thanks for the invitation," he said. "Mary and I won't be able to stay for your chili party. Although I'd prefer that to the rubber chicken we're gonna get at a charity ball later. " Lee Iacocca and his wife were led to their seats.

A biblical quotation entered my mind. "Blessed are the humble for they shall possess the land." At least for an hour and forty-eight minutes.

# BAJA 500

## Let's rent four mariachis

As a sales manager, you can turn any business trip into a boondoggle. First, see if your signs line up and your horoscope says 'just do it!' Instead, listen to Nike and just do it.

Take your sales staff on an out-of-town boondoggle with all the trimmings of a real business trip. They'll never forget it and they might re-elect you. Trips like this qualify as a sales meet-entertainment trip because it's laden with clients. Your expense reports will be stamped OK covering the $7 T&T's Tequila and Tacos, which are certified expenses. The rules tell us the T&T's are certified as long as they are consumed on foreign soil. So drink up.

The Mexican Baja is a race unlike any other. It does not, could not, resemble auto races in the United States.

It's in Ensenada, Mexico and it's off-road. Any map will tell you the Baja lies alongside the Pacific Ocean, where the Sea of Cortez wades its way almost onto the Baja race track. Follow Mexico Route 1 south to Ensinada after you leave San Diego. You make one stop and only one. Pay the first guy in uniform that stops you. Give him a twenty. If he looks disappointed give him a ten and leave, hurriedly.

Remember, you are not serious businessmen so don't dress like one Guys from IBM or P&G, still wear ties and wing-tipped shoes and have their sales meetings in Hilton or Marriot Hotels.

These killer hotels are replete with over-heated meeting rooms that seat a sales staff for eight hours every day. Each salesman is given a yellow pad. Some scratch tiny pictures onto the pad, others doodle circles and parallel lines for their psychiatrist to study, some sketch reminder notes to bring home bread and milk All leave the yellow pads behind when they leave. Cleaning women give them to their children on the first day of school.

The sales staff is allowed out for dinner but must dine within one square block of the hotel. Security Borders prevent wandering. A Sr. V.P. who has bellied-up to every bar in the Windy City shouts, "Remember gentlemen. This isn't Rush Street in Chicago. We intend to keep it that way."

No one may do anything but smoke, eat and constantly look at his watch. Junior enrollees' eyes circle the room. They feel they have finally arrived at an authentic boondoggle. The artificial palm trees have this effect. So do the panoramic wall murals of muscular Jamaican men slicing full size pineapples in one fell swoop of a machete.

Depending on the season, snow flurries outside the floor-to-ceiling walls can also shatter the dream for the youngsters until one of the hotel's lackeys starts strumming a ukulele over the hotel sound system. Elderly bridge players in the lobby mistakenly leave and prepare to retire at the sounds of the Caribbean.

With dinner consumed the heavyset men at the I.B.M. and P&G tables allow the last swallow of Mesopotamian ice cream to swim through luke warm chocolate syrup and thicken on over-taxed arteries as in a television commercial.

That's the way it is at official sales meets. Not here. The boondoggle menu for breakfast tomorrow when we check into Ensenada is Mexican eggs, sliced meat of questionable origin, putrid coffee necessarily washed down with chilled T&T's. It all mixes with the stench of determined exhaust from vehicles with serious intent.

Ensenada makes Rush Street in Chicago look like one square block outside a Hilton Hotel. Could that be one of our Detroit clients dressed in a safari outer coat with? seventeen pockets forbidden anywhere within one square block of General Motors? Let's buy him a drink.

\*   \*   \*   \*   \*   \*   \*   \*

Custom cars, off-road bikes, 4WD pick-ups, and motorcycles, plus LUV's, custom dune buggies vintage 1960's, all designed to go into the ring for longer hours than you wish, with dips and rises, flats and walls, pitfalls and deeper holes that almost reach China; all against a steel rod that was "fixed"one hour ago.

Car and Driver editors raced in the Baja 500 every year when I was publisher. They may still race in it. The Baja is a tortuous off-road race of some 432 miles from Ensenada to LaPaz. Last year's winner crossed the finish line in 8 hours, 35 minutes.

The winner averaged 50 mph on a rocky road from start to finish. Motorcycle racers hardly ever allow their bottoms to touch the seat. This is one helluva boondoggle for one prime reason. You have no responsibilities -- other then to meet, greet, and drink with clients. You are making a sales call without briefcase.

Our participation was always productive. My sales staff rubbed elbows with top-level after- market clients, some of the biggest names in industry. Our advertisers and those, who we feel, want to be our advertisers, are always in attendance. I'm talking the likes of Goodyear, Firestone, the oil companies, Fortune 500 companies that comprise a list of after-market manufacturers, who make parts race drivers would never leave home without.

These then are an important part of this gilt-edged boondoggle –clients who sip tequila or Mexican beer. Clients who prefer bowls of guacamole and crisp dippers. Only the best is reserved for advertisers in our magazine whether at the Oak Room or smack in the middle of a hell-bent desert race. .

While the magazine raced a car and participated in the off-track activities, of all the highlights after ten years' while I was with C/D, the Baja 500 took first Place.

Before my last Baja boondoggle, before I joined Psychology Today, it was agreed that "filling the gap in activity, the day before most of us left, required serious attention.

I was the senior sales guy at the time and I decided last minute to rent a nightclub, or a house, that could be converted, quickly. Waving pesos before those who could make this happen greased the wheels to get this done, and voila! a nite club appeared.

Since there was no other place to go on that needy evening we filled a glaring void. Grease monkeys rolled out from under their racecars and headed toward our club for a libation at sundown. High roller automotive and after market execs joined the crowd. Were else might a dry guy go? Elbow to elbow we filled a 2-story building. Everyone accepted our cordial invitation. In the words of an era yet to come, the Car and Driver Club rocked.

During the afternoon unbeknownst to everyone except Cookie, my east coast guy, we located the source for mariachi music and again, a deal was sealed.

After two hours of drinking and partying, my Mariachis awaited the signal to begin. Wearing Authentic Mariachi costumes, they looked magnificent.

Trumpets up! Mexican, music poured from the Sixteen Mariachis. They descended to the main Floor marching down two adjacent stone stairways, Their music exploding against concrete walls.

The musicians played to cheers of V.I.P. clients.

Many other guests, even the grease monkeys were applauding. As baskets of tacos were washed down.

Tequila and Mexican beer, the Car and Driver party was a resounding success!

Car and Driver renewed its Baja Boondoggle pledge forevermore with whomever would be their leader next time. We had reached the mandatory time to face the music. "Business," of which mucho was conducted over libations and bragging. Rep ties, buttoned down shirts, winged-tip-shoes, even kerchiefs in the proper pocket helped clad the sales staff for re-entry into a serious world of bogeys, sales goals and pocket calculators. Someone said, "the party's over" and it was

Ensenada was history. It will ring with the resonance of racecars and Mariachi music. Those who seek to stimulate the prattle of business need only turn to the joys of boondoggle.

Drive down Mexico Route 1, south, to Ensenada until you stop to pay the man. Once you hear the Mariachi Music you need do nothing but show up.

# Car Magazines- The Differences

## Car and Driver? You can hear it tickin'

My Jaguar confrontation (see Jaguar chapter) prepared me for others to come. Periodic encounters were a constant client relationships. Editors saw fit to never leave a page unturned without having an explosion occur. Actually, the magazine had little choice without duplicating the editorial style of Motor Trend and Road & Track.

Motor Trend rested comfortably in an overstuffed chair at the dining table of the Big 3 -- GM, Ford and Chrysler. Bouquets were tossed on stage at each new car introduction, almost regardless of a car's performance. MT favored what came to be known as Detroit iron and almost totally ignored the imports early on. Large wallowing Buicks come to mind when one thinks of Motor Trend. But many car buyers liked to wallow.

This suited Road & Track's founder John Bonds just fine. Bonds acted as though the Detroit automotive industry didn't exist. His magazine was practically midwife to the first imports to arrive on these shores after World War II. RT celebrated small, nimble, stiffly suspended fast, hard driving wind-in-your-face imported sports cars with the passion of a purist.

Automotive purists thrived on owning cars that went away for the weekend, sometime for weeks, staying overnight in repair shops. It was a status thing.

Ask a purist, "Where's your Peugeot?" and he might good-naturedly refer to a malfunction. Days later after parting with large sums of cash in exchange for a diagnosis – the culprit might not be found. Not to worry. He was driving as French car. The purist would later enlighten his buddies with harmless anecdotes over a bottle of Puligny Montrachet.

Car and Driver became the brash young kid on the block with an attitude. The magazine saw cars for what they were, not necessarily where they were made. The new kid on the block also had a college education. C/D became the best written, best-edited car magazine published and editorially challenged many leading general consumer magazines. And you really could hear it tickin' before you opened the brown wrapper.

# I WRITE THE PITCH SECRETLY

## And get caught re-handed!

Frank Pomerantz, VP, Sales Promotion, could con BILL Ziff with greater effect than any other employee in the company. In 1966, at least twenty-five years after Pomerantz had supposedly "tried out" for the St. Louis Browns' baseball team, Frank could still hold Ziff's undivided attention by relating his try-out experience. . "

"When I played baseball for the St. Louis Browns", was the signal for everyone else to take a short nap or slip into an extended coma. I found this incredulous but everything about Frank was incredulous.

He apparently had worked for the McCann Erickson Advertising agency, a major agency in New York, be joining Ziff. No one had any idea what Frank did at McCann.

On occasion, Frank would say, "When I was at McCann..." or, "We did that for Coca-Cola when I was at McCann. " Or "I used to meet with Jack O'Hara, McCann's CEO." When asked if he really did these things, Frank stuck to his guns  a left everyone believing he dealt only in the tr

The sales promotion department was Frank's fortress. His department churned out ongoing series of presentations for all the Ziff-Davis magazines. All of Pomerantz' work reflected his preference for graphics and not much of anything else. He never showed us a layout without saying, "And wait'll you see the graphics!"

That bothered me. I wanted more substance for Car and Driver. . We were a car magazine and I wanted an automotive presentation. I thought Frank's presentations were designed for any magazine. I had a fleeting thought that perhaps he did use the same presentation for every magazine. A tweak here, a change there, a picture flop here and voila! Who needs to write sixteen presentations? Of course, this wasn't true. At least no one said that it wasn't.

I decided I'd write my own presentation. I'd talk cars. I'd show photos or drawings of new models. Not gorgeous models with long blonde tresses flowing behind a car that's no longer in production. I didn't let Frank's extra-curricula activities with the models bother me as long as I got what I wanted. I'd write my own presentations and I'd do it secretly.

My secretary found an empty office on the sixth floor and I holed up there for an hour or two each day. Before long I had a rough outline of what I wanted. I had the promotion department run it through as just another production request – a miscellaneous job. No one would be the wiser. Or so I thought.

One late afternoon as I sat in the darkened sixth floor office reviewing my presentation slides Bill Ziff walked in. A paralysis set in. I sat as if Michelangelo bronzed me to my seat.

"Hello, Marty. Am I interrupting?" It was Bill Ziff, pleasant and cordial as always. He sat down slowly without waiting for an answer.

I had trouble speaking but managed to eek out a few words.

"Not at all, Bill. I'm just checking some slides."

"Slides," he repeated.

A one-word response. Not even a sentence. But it carried the weight of volumes. I wished I were capable of responding in kind. No matter. It would only prolong the inevitable. I'd just as soon be sentenced without trial.

"Slides for the new sales presentation. I've holed up down here for a few hours in order to concentrate. Upstairs is a zoo, as you well know. Can't get much done."

"Did Frank write this presentation?" "No, I did. "

"Let's take a look."

I set the projector on slide number one and proceeded to project the slides. Onto a small movie screen.

"Would you like me to do the commentary Bill? I'll look for my notes."

My heart was pumping and pleading that he would please say 'no' to my dimbulb suggestion. I was not capable of talking over the lump in my throat.

"Not necessary." Whew! Did I breath two lungs full!

I heard his words as a reprieve. The next ten minutes were excruciating. Slide after slide appeared on the screen. I attempted to add background on some of the slides. It was futile- - meaningless words from a nervous wreck.

"The Ford logo has to be added here, Bill. This slide is tailored for Ford." Who cares, I thought? I told myself to stop chattering. He said it wasn't necessary so just shut up! I saw an extension cord lying on the floor and thought it long enough to hang myself. Unless I already have. The last slide appeared.

"That's it, Bill. Of course it still needs a little work. But we've got time."

"Not bad. But Frank's is better. Why don't you let him do what he does best? And you do what you do best- - sell advertising. See you upstairs."

Well, I still had a job. The chairman told me to stop writing presentations. Go sell some advertising, he said. Considering the alternative, I would follow his direction. Later, I suggested to Frank that we meld our ideas using the best from each.

"That was all I was suggesting, Marty. You know I don't know a damned thing about cars. I'll do the graphics and you do the guts. And we'll have one hell of a presentation.

"Wait'll you see the shot we took of Ford's new T-Bird. Talk about graphics!!"

# ZIFF-DAVIS SALES MEETING

The atmosphere in the Ziff-Davis conference room may have been a bit tense. Our annual sales meeting was about to take place. Eight publishers sat around a table and told Ziff sales meet stories while waiting. I chimed in with one experience.

There were times when Bill Ziff, our chairman, would verbally slice a salesman conducting a sales pitch, into slender strips of flesh. Later, he'd put his arm around the salesman  (being careful not to get blood on his shirt) and accompany him back to his seat.

Eight magazine ad managers were scheduled to present their respective sales pitch to Bill Ziff. This was referred to as walking through the horrors of Bill Ziff's hell.

Ziff arrived. He surprised us when he announced a change in the game plan. He wanted the Publishers to present the sales pitch, not the ad directors, who would be scheduled next week.

I knew he carried an iniquity card in his deck. Most of us faced it before. I didn't think he'd deal it today.

Our Publishers group registered some concern. I experienced his attacks when I was a salesman, as had a few of the others. The guys who had not were in no way ready for a collision with Mr. Ziff. I've seen the best and the brightest crumble before my eyes. Burly men who wrestle inside cages for fun have been reduced to tears. Several could not continue, if permitted.

Marty Broder had recently been named the new Publisher of Hi-Fi Stereo Review. He got his baptism of slaughter last month. Ziff slammed him hard on a detail he could have let slide by. When Broder heard that the sales meet game plan changed, he felt he had somehow been booked for a return match.

Even before the change, he told us he thought of calling in sick. "Nothing serious-- perhaps cancer or something simple like an amputation--anything to get off the hook today and miraculously re--appear tomorrow in superior health."

Of a seven or eight visual board presentation, most salesmen seldom get beyond the second or third board before Ziff lowered the boom

\*     \*     \*     \*     \*     \*     \*     \*

Ziff stepped to the front of the podium. "Good morning. Let's get started. Marty, let's start with you." I thought I heard Broder exhale.

I registered shock, disbelief then a second wave of shock, as in earthquakes. I had hoped that a veteran Publisher pitched first so I'd get a feel of what Ziff was looking for. Too late for that.

"Marty will you be using slides or boards?"

"Boards. Actually, Bill, I thought of mailing it in!" My feeble attempt at humor didn't change the stoic expression on his face. A few of the Publishers giggled. Kind of helped me relax.

"OK, fire when ready," said Bill. I didn't care for his choice in words but I began.

"Today we'll be calling on Chevrolet." The Chevy pitch still felt warm from when my sales team returned after a client call last week. I hoped it had some zing left in it.

I gave my introduction to the Chevy presentation and allowed a minute for it to sink in. I addressed the first presentation board.

"Domestic automobile sales were up 9% last year. I feel your Chevrolet sales campaign will have even more clout, resulting in greater sales, if you follow the ideas I'll talk about here today.

The board pictured an assortment of current Chevy models, attractively positioned in color. "Here's your model line-up. The Chevy line with a great sales history." So far, so good, I thought.

I placed the next board on the easel. Photos of no fewer than 36 Ford, Chrysler, American Motors and import cars graced the board with the number 36, plus the words, THE COMPETITION in large bold type. I reached for a second board to place alongside the Competition board. I blocked it, deliberately. I then stepped aside for the audience to see the number 34 in big bold letters.

"There were just too many cars competing with Chevrolet to get them all on a single board, gentlemen. The type wouldn't be legible. You wouldn't see all of your competition. You might miss the total -- 70 cars compete with Chevrolet for the new car buying decision. 70 cars match Chevy's demographics,

I stepped away from the presentation boards and allowed the group to stare at car after car after car, like a thundering herd, all aimed at Chevrolet. Then I raised my voice, for effect

CAN YOU SEE YOUR COMPETITION NOW?

SIXTEEN CAR COMPANIES-- 70 DIFFERENT MODELS!

ALL TARGETING  CHEVROLET!

IT'S TIME FOR CHEVROLET TO SHOOT BACK!

(This board was most effective. I used it to talk while arranging for the next board.

Mr. Ziff stood up and challenged me. Here it comes, I thought. "Do you think Chevrolet really believes they compete with 70 other cars?"

"I sure do."

"Don't you come across as a bit of a know-it-all? Telling the great Chevrolet who sells a million cars each year that they're doing everything wrong!

"Well, I didn't exactly say that, Bill."

"No, but you certainly implied it." He seemed pissed. "How reliable is this competitive information? Did a Chevy sales manager give it to you? A friend at the agency?"

"Bill, it's information that I've read about, heard about, know to be true, and is available to everyone. These are not secrets."

"I didn't suggest they were secrets! Why isn't that new Impala not on your board?"

"Impala sells to a different market. The demographics don't match; owners are   older; less educated; new car purchase rate is too low. "

And what about those imports you show on the boards. I think you're looking for trouble. These guys hate imports.

"Bill, the sooner someone tells them the imports are coming to eat their lunch, the better off we'll all be,"

"I'm not so sure.  Didn't you tell me a Chevy manager stopped you once during your presentation and then referred to Toyota as a "toy"?"

Yes, sir. And with that kind of thinking they'll be eaten alive."

"I hope you didn't tell them that."

"If our sales staff doesn't know more than the clients, there's no purpose in calling on them. They wouldn't need us."

"How many Camaros does Chevy sell?"

I turned to pick up my copy of Automotive News.

Don't start looking things up! Tell me!"

I'd say between 300 and 400,000."

"Between? Don't you know? That's a one hundred thousand car difference. And you're supposed to know more then these men?"

He left me standing there humiliated, for what seemed a long time, my arms hanging, undecided whether to stand there or leave the platform. I left the platform.

Ziff took over, as he often does. He began to discuss the status of the automotive market reaching into areas I knew nothing about. It sounded brilliant but too esoteric. If the room were filled with eggheads it would be more apropos. I knew the audience. I didn't think there was a Chevy guy who knew what in hell Ziff was talking about.

Later, as everyone was heading to lunch, he put his arm around my shoulder. "Mart, who's the best salesman at Ziff-Davis?"

"Well it certainly isn't me, Bill. Not after that."

Anita, Ziff's secretary, said lunch was ready to be served.

"Let's have a glass of wine, Marty, and the gourmet lunch that Anita has spent all morning cooking."

"Bill, if it's okay with you, I'd like to skip it. I'm sure you understand. I'll just walk downstairs to Berger's Deli and have coffee and a bite."

That's fine. Try to get back by two o'clock, before we start again. You can help us with the others."

*   *   *   *   *   *   *   *

Rusty tends the lunch counter at Berger's Deli. She's a buxom red head who was once a size 6. One of the guys eating, whispered something in Rusty's ear. She turned, placed her hands on her hips, and said, "Pilgrim, you're too fast for me. Once I was built for speed, but now I'm built for comfort." Rusty brought me back to reality. I survived the afternoon just fine.

# JESSE K.

## Take the bus, babe!

Jessie Kadwaller fashioned a nickname for herself -- "everyone calls me Jessie K." -- as if Art really cared. When Jesse wasn't promoting her own name, she was boasting about having had lunch, or dinner and drinks with someone else's client.

Say what you will, Jesse was the top advertising salesperson at tv station NYNY in New York, beating out even those salty old sales reps who once   sold TV advertising when most people watched it through store windows.

Art was a successful, reliable magazine advertising space sales rep. He had a collection of sales awards but no one knew it.  "Everyone in space sales long enough eventually gets a trophy for showing up." That was 'Mr. Modesty' talking.

Space and broadcast reps mingled together in agency reception rooms and at Adcrafter weekly luncheons. Jesse's reputation preceded her.  Art ignored her. "She's just another mouth that drops client names like a broken bag of marbles on a New York sidewalk."

Art heard about Jesse's sales conquests long before he ever met her. They were both part of a New York advertising community where everyone knew everything about everybody else. "This town is the perfect Petri dish for the spread of gossip. If gossip was a virus, we'd all be quarantined," Art used to say.

"I may not care who all is not getting the business, but I sure as hell want to know who is, and why," he once said. "Helps me better understand a client's sales goals."

Jesse was an enterprising, but shiftless young woman who changed jobs almost as often as she changed her sheets. One day she shifted gears and Art found her in his business -- she made the quantum leap from television time sales to magazine space sales. She was the first woman to enter a business that formerly was open to men only. Jesse joined Cosmopolitan.

Had the tables been turned, most space eps wouldn't make the transfer to TV. "It's a 'promises, promises' kind of sale -- like selling he Brooklyn Bridge," they said. Space reps did not hold broadcast reps in high regard.

Costs of advertising space in a magazine appeared on the publication's rate card. Breaking the rate was unheard of. TV rates were based on market size calculation. How much time was still available as a deadline approached was a key.

"I'd rather spend time selling, than calculating," said Art.

Helen Gurly Brown was publisher of Cosmo. Brown conceived an advertising slogan for girls who read her magazine -- --Good girls go to heaven, but bad girls go everywhere. It worked.

Her slogan was tailor-made for Jesse K. and she ran with it. Jesse wore the latest fashions as advertised in her magazine thereby giving advertisers the impression that millions of readers were doing the same thing, "Talk about Cosmo's advertising effectiveness!" she'd say.

Before long, Jesse K. asked her sales manager if Cosmopolitan could offset her clothing costs. She wore three and four new outfits each week. Management quickly agreed and wondered why they hadn't thought of it sooner. Jesse was named saleswoman of the year, during her first year at the magazine. Her peers in sales agreed -- Jesse K. was some piece of work.

Resentment began to build among her colleagues, as it had at previous jobs. She always got her way with the bosses. The magazine now paid for her clothes. She never bothered calling on the younger media buyers in the ad agencies. "Who needs kids? I sell my proposals to Mr. Big over a glass of wine!"

Jessie K. pranced through the better dining establishments, draped like a trinket on her client's arm. She was sure to see the sights while the sights saw her. Jesse had the largest expense account on the staff -- and the highest income.

She earned accolades but she damaged friendships along the way. Soon too many broken promises turned everyone against her. Colleagues and clients began to see through the wrapping. It was time for Jessie K. to shift gears again.

Art remembered the first and last time he spoke directly to Jessie K. back in New York. He didn't make a very good impression. He was unaware that he'd speak with her a second time. It had been a year since he left New York. He was based in Detroit, had become successful, which surprised no one. Art was now an independent sales representative for four magazines, and he grew his business considerably during his first year.

Jessie K. called him one evening. She barely introduced herself and he hardly remembered her. She told him she had been named advertising manager of Soap Opera Digest, one of Art's magazines. In effect, Jesse K. was now one of Art's bosses.

"I'll be on the first plane to Detroit tomorrow morning. Line up some clients. You can pick me up."

Once Art realized whom he was talking to, and why, he felt as though he was losing control of the magazine. He cradled the phone between his ear and shoulder, opened the top desk drawer with one hand, and scrambled through an assortment of ball pens, rubber bands, and paper clips with the other. He finally found some Tylenol ES. He popped all four of the remaining tablets into his mouth and asked his secretary for a glass of water.

Jesse K. was spouting out orders over the telephone like an army sergeant with no regard for Art's daily sales routine. He resented her for her lack of consideration. Her words came at him like machine gun fire. As she continued, his resentment turned to dislike and would have become far more grievous had she carried on much longer.

Jesse must have sensed a fury in Art's silence. Her tone was suddenly laced with understanding.

"Promise me you won't walk too fast when you pick me up, Art." Jesse K had finally called him by name. "I'll be wearing heels and a flowered dress that I hope you like." She waited for Art to respond but he did not. "We'll be calling on k-Mart, which has huge potential. Don't you agree?"

Art had been unsuccessful calling on k-Mart. They had targeted their advertising direction to an affluent customer. k-Mart had contracted with top-line fashion agencies to model their designer clothing in ads to appear in upscale fashion magazines such as Vogue.

"I'll tell you what I think of k-Mart's strategy just as I told their top management last week.

"Trying to sell premium priced products to welfare families who depend on food stamps to eat, is insane," he told them. "Your k-Mart shopper couldn't even fit into a designer dress, let alone afford one," he continued.

As Jessie K. listened, she grew catatonic. "You told †hem that? You told them their customers were worthless?

"In so many words," Art said.

"Did you tell them that these people also buy big, new, luxury cars, which if you were doing your job, you'd also be carrying the Cadillac and Lincoln business?" Art decided he wanted no more of Jesse K. Her marketing strengths were twisted. Her personality must have been spawned in the gutter. They could never see eye over a long term. He decided to address her lack of automotive marketing knowledge.

"Big, new, luxury cars? They were probably re-possessed the same day they bought 'em! I'm surprised, since you tell me you are now an ad manager that you didn't know that our magazine's new car purchase rate is less than three percent. The lowest rate of all 2000 magazines measured!

"Which explains why I carry new car advertising from eight car divisions in all my magazines, except one," said Art. "Can you guess which one?" Silence waited for someone to speak.

"As for your planned sales trip to Detroit, be prepared to land at Detroit Metro at 8 am. That's when the first flight of the day arrives. I know this because I've picked up my other publishers many times when they arrive one week after they call me, not the night before."

Art decided he'd package everything she wanted in a nice, neat bag and have it waiting for her upon arrival. Then he spoke.

"I suggest you walk slowly, since you'll be wearing heels. Go to the luggage area. Rent a pull cart for two dollars, quarters only, please. Take the down elevator to the bus station which is across the street," Art continued. "I'm not really certain. I haven't been on a bus since I was twelve. Nor have any of my publishers." He waited for an interruption but there was none.

"Direct the driver to take you to k-Mart. The people on the bus will be going with you since their 'big, beautiful luxury cars' have likely been re-possessed. Should you require a bag carrier, I would expect anyone on board would carry your bag for a dollar or two.

"You'll have all of these supports waiting for you when you arrive at the gate.

"But you won't have me."

Click.

# AMERICAN MOTORS

## Where did McNealy come from?

My Jaguar confrontation prepared me for others to come.

Periodic encounters were a constant in my client relationships because of our editorial independence. Actually, the magazine had little choice without duplicating the other car books.

Car and Driver saw cars for what they were, not necessarily where they were made. The new kids on the block, our readers, had a college education. C/D became the best written, best-edited car magazine published and editorially challenged many leading general consumer magazines.

Unfortunately, the mindset of our editorial side was In conflict with this formula for excellence. If a car didn't measure up our subscribers knew it the moment they heard the new issue tick.

My sales responsibilities were expanded during the 1960's and I was named Advertising Director. I found myself calling on Detroit's Big 3, men from GM, Ford and Chrysler who for the most part were big guys, tall and often brawny.

This was a shock after spending two years calling on downsized versions of men whose European factories made small Fiats, MG's and V W 's. The Cadillac sales manager, in jest, reminded me that his Eldorados measured nineteen feet long.

During a major sales presentation before American Motors' top marketing and ad agency personnel sixteen client and agency people showed up to listen. I was delighted with the turnout. Then Bill McNealy, president of AMC, surprised me when he walked in. Presidents rarely attended media sales presentations. I felt flattered having only met him briefly once or twice. I should have known better.

McNealy remained quiet during most of my presentation while others asked questions and appeared to be supportive of my suggestions. I had gotten to know three or four of them previously. I felt good about my performance. Maybe McNealy's presence made me try a little harder. He had a reputation for being brash and outspoken. I knew he wasn't there to kill time but I didn't know he was there to kill me.

As McNealy sat in the back of the room I summarized all of the sales points, solid reasons AMC should increase its advertising budget in C/D. Suddenly McNealy stood up and interrupted me. A quiet fell over the room. He then pounced like a lion from his lair and proceeded to nullify everything I had said during the prior fifteen minutes. It was a crippling moment I'll never forget. I thought it best to stand there and take it.

Car and Driver's writers constantly called AMC cars a Nash, a much earlier AMC car that the car company wanted to forget. It was referred to in a denigrating and sometimes humorous manner. AMC was in the process of unsaddling itself from the Rambler image of an old lady's car. C/D poked fun at the Rambler, if it mentioned it at all.

We said that AMC's Gremlin could have been successful in a cartoon environment. The lines of the car begged for a mustache, oversize glasses "and a doofy little cap".

"The poor little ant-eater didn't know what it was or what it wanted to be," said C/D in a road test.

The Javelin, a new sports car designed to compete with Ford's Mustang, was hot. In fact, under McNealy's direction, the Javelin went road racing -- a major step and a costly one designed to put AMC on the map with performance cars and rid it of its sorry image. Car and Driver supported AMC in its endeavor for the first time. But it was too late. McNealy was on the attack. His guns were loaded.

"You're standing here touting the merits of your rag, when you're no different from any other car magazine," he said. "If we give you the advertising business you still don't give us a favorable road test. If we don't give you the business, we get bad road tests anyway. So what the hell are you trying to sell us here?"

The meeting room turned stone cold silent. Yet the impact of his high-pitched voice seemed to reverberate like a succession of facial punches. His final, and I hoped it was a final Admonishment seemed to have been targeted at me, personally.

I did stand alone at the head of the room facing the audience And asked for more business. In a sense I was practically being held responsible for AMC' s product critique, rightly or wrongly.

I was stunned. His staff and members of his ad agency sat quiet This was no time to take sides.

I thought of a dozen responses but he was, after all, the president. I felt empathy from the entire room. He wasn't through.

"Big 3?" he continued. "What about Big 4?" I had referred to the Big 3 during my pitch. The title has been accepted around the world. "Your magazine treats our products like a joke. And you're here asking for more business? Give me a break!"

He stormed from the room.

I went to lunch alone. I had to cancel the large luncheon planned in another AMC meeting room. Most apologized for their boss' behavior and excused themselves from lunch with apologies that was understandable.

Months went by. His staff knew that C/D was an important part of AMC's marketing plan. So did McNealy. They waited as I did. He later approved only part of my proposal as though the incident had never occurred. I waited it out hoping to re-build the relationship as I had done with Jaguar.

A few more months later I called McNealy, direct. He planned to attend the New York Auto Show. I was still based in NYC. I was surprised he took the call. I invited him to dinner in NYC while he was in town for †he Auto Show

He asked me to pick him up t the Essex House on Central Park South a short distance from the Coliseum, site of the auto show. When I arrived he asked me what I'd like to drink.

"A cold beer would hit the spot. Thanks."

"Why don't we just have a couple and grab a hot dog on the way to the show?" he asked. I was ready to eat green molded bread dipped in acid if that's what it took.

Beer and hot dogs were classic McNealy. Not that he didn't dine in the Oak Rooms of the world. He didn't always want to. He was one tough out-spoken s.o.b. But I iiked him anyway. .

We walked the short distance to the Coliseum in a light rain. McNealy stopped at a curbside hot dog stand. We stood together under the vendor's bright umbrella.

"You take mustard?" he asked. I heard a chorus of angels sing as a relationship plank fell into place.

# SPECIAL INTERESTS

## Motorcycles

Bill Ziff explained one of the qualities of a special interest magazine. He said the editorial content serves as a screen to attract readers genuinely interested in the magazine's subject matter. It quickly came to my attention that most of the work force at Ziff Davis was there for the same reason.

Until I joined Ziff Davis I thought that anyone who rode a motorcycle was daffy. Chris Farrell, and me a high school buddy. would ride to Harlem to hear Billie Holiday sing "Lover Man". It still sounded good playing on a worn out juke turntable. We couldn't hear it anywhere else from the Bronx to forever. Besides, it gave me an excuse to ride the bike.

One evening, just as we dropped another ten nickels
In the jukebox, a policeman came in. He walked toward
Christy and me. Since it was an all-black bar we assumed he
was arresting one of them. He wasn't.

"I want you two guys to saddle up and ride your
horse back to the Bronx the same way you came in. They
don't want you here, you don't belong here, and I'm
certain you both are bright enough to never return."

Later, I had other opportunities to ride. I stretched a weeklong sales trip to the Los Angeles area and stayed the weekend. Some bike and car magazine guys I compete with on weekdays invited me to go dirt biking. They were Motor Trend and Cycle World guys. They assumed this Car and Driver guy from back east lived the same way they do. Play on weekends, play on weekdays, play whenever the sun is out and it almost never sets out there.

We had ten guys and two wives, all of whom were about 30 years old. I was 50. They all wore "Sons of Thunder" tee shirts with lightning bolts on the back. I had to re-wear a button down blue oxford business shirt I made sales calls in the week before. Given the choice to either bike ride or stop for rolls and buns after mass was a no-brainer. I was home for the weekend.

My sojourn began Sunday morning. I managed my Honda 100 yards to the top of a hill, clearly the entrance to L.A. 98. I felt like I was about to make my first sky dive. I was later informed that Rt. 98 was the most treacherous freeway in L.A. Motorists drive 150 to 200 mph on Sundays to "get even" for having to drive between 2 and 3 mph to work all week long.

It took me one and one-half hours to finally enter L.A 98
as flocks of unleashed cars flew by apparently with no
intention of ever stopping again. I guessed it would take me
at least 7 seconds to board Rt. 98, throw it into high gear
without getting hit in the doofus. I had the very next car
pegged at arriving in 5 seconds. That's all she wrote.

One guy's poison is another guy's luck. Suddenly

Sixteen cars crashed, a telescoped pile-up, piles of wreckage left a small path to maneuver onto the freeway before all hell broke lose again.

I found the exit where the dirt bikers ride. There were the expected welcome sighs of relief from my guys. Some said they ride Rt. 98 every Sunday, "for the fun of it".

Two bikers tore down to the bottom of the downhill dirt slope, launched as if they had rockets on board, and flew through the air to somewhere. "There goes Charlie and Rob," said one. "Let's go, we're next!" he shouted, to no one in particular. They were doing what they like to do. I found a mound and sat for a while. Gave me time to choose between church and dirt biking.

I could smell the rolls and buns.

# I'm Appointed Ad Manager

## Has anyone seen my staff?

David E. Davis Jr. asked me to sit in on a budget meeting with he and Tom Sargeant, ad manager of Car and Driver. I had been an advertising salesman for less than one year. At the conclusion of the meeting, Davis sprung it on me.

"How would you like to be advertising manager of Car and Driver?" I let out a loud questionable "what?" I thought it might be a joke. confounded, confused and almost numb as tho my dentist shot me full f Novocain. I felt as if I was just asked to walk into the lobby of the Waldorf-Astoria Hotel and start to manage it. Or enter the subway, commandeer a subway train and drive it back and forth through Manhattan, Brooklyn, Queens and the Bronx, maybe picking up passengers when I could stop the s.o.b. I would be expected to do this without a moment's training. That's how I felt about managing C/D.

Tom said, "Just say 'yes', Mart." He put his arm around me and laughed out loud. "I think we caught him off guard, Dave."

Tom Sargeant was about to be named advertising manager of Cycle magazine in California. He was leaving Car and Driver.

I had no idea who Tom's replacement would be. My best guess would have been T.C. Browne. I had been hired less than one year earlier as a sales rep under Tom. I was still wet behind the ears.

"Tom thinks you're ready. So do I," said Davis.

"Well, I am surprised. I'm not going to say 'no'. But I am going to ask, how does one go about managing a sales staff? I've never done it before. Incidentally, where is the sales staff?

The long litany of zeros began with David E. "Well, we're going into the minus column before we get to he plus column." I told him I was confused. ""I'm not surprised, Martin Thomas. T.C. Browne, who was to be on your staff, is returning to la-la land to replace our Los Angeles guy who's leaving for greener pastures," said Davis. "T.C. has driven us nuts with his complaints about New York weather. Once an Angelino always an Angelino. At least in his case. "I'm perfectly content living in Brooklyn Heights, walking through snow and slush," said Davis. "T.C. hates it in spite of the new galoshes I bought him."

"You gave him new galoshes? You sure take care of your own Dave," I said.

"I tried everything else to get him to make sales calls, T.C. has a fetish for fine shoes. Spends a fortune on them. He refuses to walk in anything that's even ∂amp. He never leaves the office when it rains. I'm surprised he even shows up when it snows. He orders take out food when it does."

"Have you seen the galoshes sitting on his desk, Dave?" said Tom. "He fills 'em with oranges to remind himself of California. He told me he conducted a survey of his Los Angeles friends to find out if any of them knew what galoshes were. Offered one of our nifty Car and Driver calendars as a prize. Nobody won!"

"You see Martin Thomas," said Davis. "You never can tell what's gonna happen next. You came to this meeting a lowly salesman and your leaving as sales manager by God!"

"What's a sales manager without a sales staff," I asked.

"Mere details, kind sir," said Davis in one of his best W.C. Fields impersonations. "You'll have to beat 'em away with a large stick once word gets out. I promise."

I walked back to my office and called Maureen. We talked about my promotion and the sudden turn of events. One year ago I slogged jobless through that same snow and slush that T.C. Browne can't stand. Now I'll be interviewing guys in the same predicament. I hoped the threatening weather would hold off and the subterranean goons wouldn't go on strike again.

Davis, leaving the building for Europe, popped his head through my door." We once did have a sales staff. Tom favored one bright young man who decided he wanted to star on Broadway and left. He hasn't been heard from since. Two months ago there was Jim Vaughn, who just as TC has a fetish for California, Jim told us he had, n so many words, a fetish for the Catholic Church.

*   *   *   *   *   *   *   *

Monday morning brought more surprises.  Advertising Age,. The national trade paper, told its readers of my good fortune. The N.Y. Times called.  They wanted to know how old I was and where I went to college. Irwin Danis, the ZD office manager wanted to know if I wanted a new couch. Tom was taking his to California. I told Irwin "yes".

I was finally alone. I looked around for sales call book and found it. Someone was to call on Jaguar next Monday. I guess that meant me. I had time, either to hang myself, or find out where Jaguar was located. I stopped Davis, the only one left, as he stepped onto the elevator.

"Dave, where is Jaguar located?"

"Jaguar is located on the corner of 57th Street and Sixth Avenue next to Carnegie Hall. Unfortunately, our new issue should be out by the time you call on them. Poor timing but I guess it has to be done sooner or later.

"We road tested their new XKE. It flopped. I believe Pat Bedard who tested their car said Jaguar should have the decency to leave the car business. He said when we uncovered a stone, we found another stone. You'll have to read the test before you go anywhere near Mr. Johannes Erdman, the temperamental Dutchman who rules the roost for Jaguar throughout the United States send Canada."

I started to experience the sensation of the word ticking and hoped it wasn't followed by an explosion on my very first sales call as ad manager.

# Christmas Party

## The kids welcome royalty

Anne Marie allowed Tim to open our entrance door. Terrence received permission to close it. A red-haired man with thick traces of bright gray on the sides entered. He was of medium height and wore a fluffed handlebar mustache over a broad smile. Graham Whitehead, top Brit in America and lord and master over the sale of every MG, Triumph and Rover in the United States, had indeed arrived.

Under direction from Anne Marie, the CEO of British Leyland Motors carefully handed over his outer coat to Christine, his hat to Patty, his gloves to Tim and his scarf to Terrence. All four kids hung the clothing in the hallway closet then stood staring at Mr. Whitehead.

"What a marvelous reception, dear Marty. Nothing short of the fuss that was made when I knelt before the Queen." He laughed at his own joke. Chuck Curpier, Publisher of Car and Driver and my boss, greeted Graham and proceeded to walk with him into the living room. A catering person awaited drink orders much to Mr. Whitehead's delight. I was happy that Graham saw fit to attend our party. He was the largest imported car advertiser in our magazine. It was the perfect way to begin what I hoped would be a perfect evening.

No sooner had the entrance door closed than the doorbell rang again. The party was underway. The kids were getting the hang of it and took their positions. The children who stood with puzzled looks on their faces met Mr. Frederico Bellini, U.S. President of the Fiat Motor Company. Senor

Bellini chose to leave his coat and hat in his car. "He doesn't even have a scarf," whispered Patty who was nudged from the rear by Christine.

The entry assignments went fairly smooth. The kids received the arriving guests. Chuck greeted guests individually and led them inside to meet other Officers of various imported car companies. The waitress seemed to depart and re-appear, on cue, out of nowhere usually with fresh drink orders on her tray. This time she served gorgonzola cream puffs that Senor Bellini took to with a passion.

Maureen and I had recently returned from a European business-pleasure vacation and Bellini had arranged with Milano, Fiat's headquarters in Europe, to provide my wife and I with a car. A full size sedan, a model not yet sold in the U.S., awaited us at the Rome airport. When we arrived at Milano to visit the Fiat people, I was gifted with a leather briefcase; Maureen received a necklace and a bracelet, which she adored; boxes of candy for the kids back home, and the offer to keep the car for as long as we were in Europe. We were happy to renew acquaintance with Senor Bellini.

One of the kids, perhaps Patty, called to my attention the man who sat in the den since his arrival. I recognized him as Jean-Martin Devereux, President of Peugeot, the French car company. He had been listening to the classical guitar player we retained, since he arrived. "Maybe he doesn't know anyone, Dad. Is that why he's sitting alone?" Patty felt sorry for him. I went into the den, introduced myself since I didn't know him that well either, and sat with Monsieur Devereux.

I told him how we decided to choose the classical guitar player from a variety of music choices. He obviously was pleased with our selection. He said that he and the musician had discussed the content of the music earlier. I was glad we followed the recommendation of the high school student we conferred with. If Monsieur Devereux enjoyed the music, that's all that mattered as far as business was concerned.

Editor Bob Brown and two members of his editorial staff arrived without jackets but their sweaters looked presentable. Chuck stood with them for several minutes probably to insure that they would socialize with the men whose cars they write about rather than stand on the periphery of the party, which is probably what they preferred to do. They seemed more interested in food and welcomed a waitress as she stood dutifully with a tray full of crab canapés.

When the latecomers arrived I was standing at the far end of the living room. I couldn't see who they were because of the crowd guests in the living room. I wouldn't have been able to get through anyway. I decided I'd greet them as the evening wore on.

Christine told me that the coat closet was filling up. "Squeeze the coats together, Chris." She squeezed them as tight as she could and got more hangars from her mother's closet. Chris rushed out of the foyer toward the coat closet and then dashed madly up the stairs. Christine was on a mission.

I struck up a conversation with Georges Basilou, President of Renault, whom I saw regularly. His offices in Englewood were just fifteen minutes from my home. I'd find all kinds of reasons just to stop by and build relationships with he and his staff.

My wife crossed the room and joined the Frenchman and me. She knew Monsieur Basilou from the first class trip Renault had packaged together to introduce the new Renault R-5 to the press. The unveiling was held at the Silverado Country Club in Napa Valley, California.

"Bonjour, Monsieur Basilou. We're so glad you could come."

"Mrs. Toohey, your husband told me your party wouldn't be the same without me. He is always his usual charming self," said Basilou, smiling.

I secretly hoped that my supposed charm might increase the amount of advertising Renault would place in Car and Driver during the coming year.

Bob Brown began to approach our group but once he saw who we were talking to he turned on his heel and went in an opposite direction. Apparently Brown had enough of Basilou after our last meeting with him.

An earlier issue of Car and Driver carried a highly critical road test of the Renault R-5. Since my wife and I accepted a 5-day California press junket as guests of Renault, the timing could not have been worse. Upon our return I insisted that Brown join me and call upon Basilou to at least explain the reasons why the editorial staff felt that the car had so many shortcomings.

Basilou appreciated the call but still believed that the car was dealt with harshly. Thankfully, Renault did not cut or reduce their advertising in our magazine, a strategy other advertisers used in the past to "teach a lesson". Small wonder that Brown saw fit to correct his course across the room.

Maureen accepted compliments from guests who said they were impressed with the décor of our home. Several gathered before the imposing Victorian staircase, at the center of the foyer. The quarter oak stairway, with its handrails and supporting posts, took my wife and I countless evenings and weekends in order to strip the 100-year-old staircase down to the original raw wood.

Maureen's father discovered a gun shop that sold a varnish used primarily for the stocks of rifles. We applied the gunstock varnish to the banisters and the decorative balustrades. The results were exceptional.

Gertrude McWilliams, vice-president of the Rover Car Company, exclaimed, "The staircase is simply outstanding. It appears to be one large piece of beautiful furniture. Wouldn't you agree, Bruce?" Mrs. McWilliams was addressing her husband. Mr. and Mrs. McWilliams ran the Rover Car Company from their offices in Manhattan and spoke with British accents.

Graham Whitehead had taken note of the paneling in the den where the classical guitarist played. "What kind of wood is that paneling made of, Marty?" I told him the wood was antique birch and had to be purchased in four by twelve foot panels to accommodate the nine-foot ceilings in our house. He seemed impressed which caused me to be flattered considering the decor of the home a man of his position would probably live in.

A waitress stopped before us. She presented a tray of what she called asparagus and prosciutto bundles. They were mouth watering Maureen always made a family favorite at holiday time – asparagus and cream cheese wrapped in toasted white cheese bread. We didn't have a name for it. I thought for futures we might call them bundles.

"Well no wonder this is such a great party. Look who the host is!" I spotted Jack Reilly wending his way through a roomful of guests.

Jack was one of my favorite people in the business. Jack could stand penniless and in rags in the middle of an empty boulevard. In a matter of moments every woman above the age of sixteen would flock to him. That's how good- looking this guy was. Jack Reilly was Executive Vice-President of the Porsche Division of Volkswagen. He ranked just under the CEO of VW, the parent company.

Jack was instrumental in convincing Volkswagen dealers nationwide that in order to represent Porsche they had to build separate dealer showrooms to house and sell the luxury car, a considerable investment. Heaven forbid the Beetle dealer show a Porsche on the same showroom floor next to a VW that cost one-fifth as much.

Jack addressed the small group we were talking to. "If any of you ever decide to freshen up your wardrobe, Marty here is just your guy." I knew what was coming. Months earlier Jack complimented me on a black and white hounds tooth suit I was wearing that my wife picked out. It became my favorite suit in the closet and I wanted to wear it every day. Jack took note of it during a presentation I conducted for him and his advertising staff in the Porsche meeting rooms.

Before I knew it he had me in his Porsche 911 heading downtown to Seventh Avenue and Seventeenth Street to Barney's, "The Only Store Of Its Kind" as the radio advertising exclaimed. Jack tore through the suit racks like a starving man of skin and bone.

"Every time I see a suit I want to buy I find another one that's even nicer." Jack wound up buying three suits and I forget how many shirts and ties. He said that he felt as though he had died and went to heaven.

"Marty, I don't know how to thank you. This is the greatest

Shopping experience I've ever had."

"I'm glad you feel that way, Jack. Twenty minutes ago you looked like a slob." We both howled at my comment.

Jon Petersen, Marketing Director of Saab, the Swedish car company, was placing an hors d'ouevre in his mouth when I approached him.

"Don't stop because of me, Jon. I just wanted to see if you ever come up for air!"

"Please don't interrupt me, Marty. Allow me to pig out. These hors d'ouevres are fantastic. I've been making a meal out of them."

"Well that's what's expected, Jon. We're not serving you dinner, too! This is a cocktail party. Just booze and finger food."

"Sounds good to me, Mart. I'm a nut for goat cheese. Your outstanding kitchen staff have mixed it with artichoke and spread it on bruschetta. Dee-lish! My compliments to whomever is preparing this food." He swallowed hard. I asked your dutiful waitress to package a large box of those black truffle canapés for me, but I'm sure she knew I was just kidding." He took a final bite. "Not if she knows you as well as I do!"

Jon had demonstrated the 4-cylinder Saab for me in the company's parking lot the previous winter. The snow was deep.

It was a front-drive car that mixed the oil and gas together the way one would with an outboard motor. This was obviously seen as a negative in the sales department especially competing head-on with Volvo, the other Swede in the industry.

No one from Volvo had accepted our invitation. Apparently there was a conflict on their calendar.

Daughter Christine caught my attention long enough to tell me that a young woman named Caroline, from our magazine, had just dropped an ash from her cigarette on our living room rug and burned a hole in it. I asked Chris to make certain the burn had extinguished and that I'd handle it later.

Graham Whitehead approached me. He was the first one to arrive and it appeared he would be the first one to leave. He was holding his outercoat and his hat. Apparently the kids were doing their job.

"Marty, my experience as a guest in your home these past few hours has been nothing short of joyful – and as for your home it is truly elegant. Thank you so much for having me."

Guests formed what almost resembled a reception line to thank me and Maureen for the evening. Others milled about the foyer, waiting patiently for the kids to locate and return coats and hats and gloves and scarves to their proper owners. Before long the house was ours again. I turned toward Maureen.

"Well, Mrs. Toohey. Whadda ya think?" Maureen thought for a moment. "If we do it again next year, we'll need a bigger coat closet."

# Jim Claar

## Where'd this guy come from?

As children we played the game of musical chairs. Miss the chair and you landed on your derriere. We still play as adults only the stakes are higher. Miss the chair and your career can go up in smoke.

David E. Davis, Jr. changed chairs in 1978. He left Car and Driver and jumped into the creative director's chair at Campbell-Ewald Advertising in Detroit. He went on to write many Chevrolet ads and then changed chairs again. He enjoyed more success in the publishing business with another car magazine after convincing media mogul Rupert Murdoch to start a car magazine called Automobile. It still is a success today.

Davis' replacement came from a Washington D.C. company that published trade publications serving the military, aviation and defense industries. Jim Claar left his position as advertising director of Missiles and Rockets Magazine, which in retrospect should have told us something. He changed chairs and became Publisher of Car and Driver. We got him.

When Claar was officially introduced to the editorial staff he concluded the meeting with two requests. "Make deadline and make budget and you'll have no problems with me," according to Editor Gordon Jennings. "He never asked anything about the magazine," said Gordon. "I don't think he knows diddley about car magazines. Didn't ask a single question. He's just another suit."

I was advertising manager at the time. When Claar met our advertising sales staff he repeated the same strategy. He left us with two requests which could have sounded like mandates. "Make sales calls and make budget." The meeting left us with as many unanswered questions about Claar's qualifications as we had before we met him. He remained an enigma as long as he remained our publisher.

My Detroit manager, Robert U. Brown, suffered from a paranoia that surfaced whenever changes in Ziff-Davis took place; especially if they effected him directly. Brown had established a comfortable relationship with David E. Davis and Bill Ziff long before I came on the scene. He traded upon it with their permission. They listened patiently to his dismay and discontent when I was named ad manager Brown thought he should have gotten the job.

When Brown got through excavating truckloads of first impressions of Jim Claar, all bad, from his circle of gossip-mongers he almost fell to his paranoid knees. Since I dealt with Claar on a day-to-day basis Brown tried to cultivate me as his point man. My "reports" enabled him to determine a measuring stick of anxiety for the day. Reassuring as I tried to be I sensedl his thumb was always on the panic button.

When Chevrolet won Car and Driver's "Car of the Year" award for its new Corvette, Bob Lund, general manager of the division, was kind enough to invite me to make the presentation at his division's black tie dinner during the National Automobile Dealers Association (NADA) Convention.

We'd all be present the following week in New Orleans. It worked perfectly since Brown would be present as our Detroit man, and Claar would have the opportunity of meeting Chevrolet's mucky-mucks. I'd have Claar make the presentation to Bob Lund who was happy to go along with my suggestion.

"I understand your taking the spotlight off yourself Marty and having it shine on your new publisher," he said. "That's what I'd do. Hope this fellow Claar appreciates it. You'd go a long way at General Motors," he laughed.

With Chevrolet photographers at the ready, its public relations machine set to grind out front page news stories and pictures for the trade press. It didn't get any better for the new boy on the block. Claar seemed to agree when I told him about the plan. .

Brown and I spent the afternoon of the Chevrolet dinner party touring the convention floor introducing Claar to as many people as possible. Conventions are wonderful baptisms of fire for anyone new to the business because they get to meet so many clients so quickly. Tired and dragging by mid-afternoon with a long evening ahead we took a cab to our hotel and made plans for the evening during the cab ride.

"Let's meet in my room at five o'clock," I said. "We'll run through a brief presentation rehearsal and leave for the Chevrolet dinner at around six.

To get each of us in on the presentation act I'd like to have you open Bob. Throw out some frivolous or humorous remarks, at which you excel, and turn the podium over to me for a short word or two. I'll introduce Jim, "fresh from his new post in New York as publisher of Car and Driver!" Drum roll, ta-dah and all that jazz.

"Jim, you've probably awarded golden missiles and rockets to dozens of generals at Washington D.C. black tie dinners so I'll leave it to you to say whatever you think appropriate," I said. I didn't feel comfortable telling the publisher what to say.

"What did you say is the name of the car?" said Jim. We laughed together.

"Just don't say 'Vega' " said Bob.

"Did you guys know I drive a Corvette?" said Jim.

"Great segue, Jim," I said. "Tell 'em you bought it because you knew you were going to work for Car and Driver." The cab deposited the three of us at the hotel and we made Jim pay the driver.

"You make more money then we do," said Bob. Everyone laughed.

\* \* \* \* \* \* \* \*

My hotel doorbell rang promptly at 5. It was Bob. "Where's Jim?" he asked.

"Probably on his way," I said.

"How do you think the afternoon went?" Bob asked.

"Like most afternoons at conventions. What do you mean?"

"Jim seemed a little stilted. I couldn't tell if he's just nervous or so relaxed he doesn't give a rat's ass for any of this."

"Did you bring that anxiety button with you Bob? You promised me you'd leave it home."

"He's a hard guy to get to know, Mart. You're with him every day but I haven't had more than a passing conversation with him since we arrived yesterday. We spent the entire evening together at dinner last night. He still doesn't know me and I sure don't know him."

"Well he did spend time talking to our guests which is what one is supposed to do especially when they're clients, Bob."

"Yeah. Telling those dumb ass jokes. The guy from Ford must have asked him three times about Missiles and Rockets and he just skirted the answer each time."

"What are you saying, Bob? Jim just landed for cryin' out loud. He's been dumped into a strange kettle of automotive fish and he's learning to swim all over again. How do you think you or I would have held up today if we were the new boy on the block at a military convention?"

"We've both been there, Mart. And we'd both do better than he did today."

My telephone rang. It was Jim.

"Hey, buddy. This is Jim. I hate to disappoint but I'm not going to be able to make it tonight. Must've been the hot dogs we had at the convention. I'm not a bit concerned though. You guys are pros. Go make us look good. See you in the morning. I'm going back to bed." I hung up.

"Jim's not coming," said Brown.

"That's what he said, Bob."

"Was he drunk?"

"I don't think so. Hard to say. Didn't talk that much, really."

"I'll bet he was drunk."

"What makes you say that?"

"Heard it through my grapevine ."

"Your circle of fear and paranoia?"

"More than once."

"Well, as I was saying a couple of hours ago, why don't we have you open the proceedings with some frivolous remarks. Make us laugh, Bob. Especially you and me. We really need a good laugh. Then introduce me, tell 'em what a great guy I am. Then I'll present the award to Bob Lund. And then the two of us will get drunk.

"Oh, by the way, what's the name of the car?" We laughed nervously as we left the hotel. We timed the drinks perfect;y. "

# I Quietly Write the Pitch

## And get caught re-handed!

Frank Pomerantz, VP Sales Promotion, could con BILL Ziff with greater effect than any other employee in the company. In 1966, at least twenty-five years after Pomerantz had supposedly "tried out" for the St. Louis Browns' baseball team, Frank could still hold Ziff's undivided attention by relating his try-out experience. . "

"When I played baseball for the St. Louis Browns", was the signal for everyone else to take a short nap or slip into an extendedcomIfound this incredulous but everything about Frank was incredulous.

He apparently had worked for McCann Erickson Advertsising agency in New York, before joining Ziff. No one had any idea what Frank did at McCann.

On occasion, Frank would say, "When I was at McCann..." or, "We did that for Coca-Cola when I was at M cCann. " Or "I used to meet with Jack O'Hara, McCann's CEO." When asked if he really did these things, Frank stuck to his guns  a left everyone believing he dealt only in the tr

The sales promotion department was Frank's fortress.  His department churned out ongoing series of presentations for all the Ziff-Davis magazines. All of Pomerantz' work reflected his preference for graphics and not much of anything else. He never showed us a layout without saying, "And wait'll you see the graphics!"

That bothered me. I wanted more substance for Car and

Driver. We were a car magaziand I wanted an automotive presentation. I thought Frank's presentations were designed for any magazine. I had a fleeting thought that perhaps he did use the same presentation for every magazine. A tweak here, a change there, a picture flop here and voila! Who needs to write sixteen presentations?

Of course, his wasn't true. At least no one said that it wasn't.

I decided I'd write my own presentation. I'd talk cars. I'd show photos or drawings of new models. Not gorgeous models with long blonde tresses flowing behind a car that's no longer in production. I didn't let Frank's extra-curricula activities with the models bother me as long as I got what I wanted. I'd write my own presentations and I'd do it secretly.

My secretary found an empty office on the sixth floor and I holed up there for an hour or two each day. Before long I had a rough outline of what I wanted. I had the promotion department run it through as just another production request – a miscellaneous job. No one would be the wiser. Or so I thought.

One late afternoon as I sat in the darkened sixth floor officreviewing my presentation slides Bill Ziff walked in A paralysis set in. I sat as if Michelangelo bronzed mto my seat. "Hello, Marty. Am I interrupting?" It was Bill Ziff, pleasant and cordial as always. He sat downslowly without waiting for an aI had trouble speaking but managed to eek out a few words.

"Not at all, Bill. I'm just checking some slides."

"Slides," he repeated.

A one-word response. Not even a sentence. But it carried the weight of volumes. I wished I were capable of responding in kind. No matter. It would only prolong the inevitable. I'd just as soon be sentenced without trial.

"Slides for the new sales presentation. I've holed up down here for a few hours in order to concentrate. Upstairs is a zoo, as you well know. Can't get much done."

"Did Frank write this presentation?" "No, I did. "

"Let's take a look. I set the projector on slide number one and proceeded to project the slides onto a small movie screen.

"Would you like me to do the commentary Bill? I'll look for my notes."

My heart was poundng and pleading that he would please se ay no' to my dimbulb suggestion. I was not capable of talking over the lump in my throat.

"Not necessary." Whew! I breathed with both lungs.

I heard his words as a reprieve. The next ten minutes were excruciating. Slide after slide appeared on the screen. I attempted to add background on some of the slides. It was futile- - meaningless words from a nervous wreck.

"The Ford logo has to be added here, Bill. This slide is tailored for Ford." Who cares, I thought? I told myself to stop chattering. He said it wasn't necessary so just shut up! I saw an extension cord lying on the floor and thought it long enough to hang myself. Unless I already have. The last slide appeared.

"That's it, Bill. Of course it still needs a little work. But we've got time."

"Not bad. But Frank's is better. Why don't yeou let Frank  dwhat he does best? And you do what you do best- -sell ladvertising. See you upstairs."

Well, I still had a job. The chairman told me to let Frank  writet he esentations.. "Go sell some advertising", he said. Considering the presentattions I would follow his direction. Later, I suggested to Frank that we meld our ideas using the best from each.

"That was all I was suggesting, Marty. You know I don't know a damned thing about cars. I'll do the graphics and you do the guts. And we'll have one hell of a presentation.

"Wait'll you see the shot we took of Ford's new T-Bird.

Talk about graphics!!"

# ADIOS, MR. PUBLISHER

This was in late February 1976. It started to snow. Brad Briggs, Ziff-Davis Vice Chairman, asked me to stop by his office. Somehow I didn't feel good vibes about the call.

I hadn't received a vacation card from him in the ten years I was with Car and Driver. I got one yesterday mailed from France. What's changed? Brad and I were business-close, but hardly personal- close.

It occurred to me that I had just completed my tenth year at ZD and was now fully vested. That was hardly relevant although I had witnessed a few sorry souls cleaning out their desk on their auspicious day- becoming vested in the ZD retirement plan and getting fired the same say.

I got off the elevator and walked the length of a long hall. Bill Ziff's office was straight ahead. Brad's was next to his. The walk seemed unusually quiet. There was a wandering mail boy delaying his return to the mailroom and his boss. . I did that ten years ago.

I expected to see Ann Kojas, Ziff's secretary and a good friend at her desk. Not there. Judy Hitchcock, my promotion lady, who I traveled with, laughed with and listened to her recite tales of her love life, wasn't there. I bet they knew why Briggs wanted to see me.

With nothing more to go on than my vesting date and a meaningless greeting card I walked into Brad's office and we shook hands. It didn't take Brad long to get down to business.

"There's something I want to talk to you about, Mart. It has to do with you continuing as Publisher of Car and Driver."

Bingo! There it was! I was about to be fired! But why?

"Bill (Ziff) wanted to sit in on this meeting but he's preparing to leave town." I was disappointed that Bill didn't fire me. Instead, he left it to his number one man.

I was the only salesman Ziff ever trained – hourly meetings once a week. Other ZD salesmen were jealous. I barely noticed. I didn't know any better. "He's never even said hello to me," was a common plaint from several salesmen. . I eventually realized I probably spent more time being interviewed by Ziff for the job than others spent in a decade.

*    *    *    *    *    *    *    *

As time passed and I now had dozens of sales alls under my belt, Ziff would, on occasion, slice me to ribbons when I conducted a presentation at a sales meet. He'd find fault with so many things I was saying that when he finally got through there was little left of me. I'd feel hollow inside standing alone on a platform, our sales staff looking mournfully at me, Ziff battering me with criticism.

I remember on one occasion getting up at 4 am to take one more look at my sales pitch, just in case. Sure enough Ziff invited himself to our Publishers Meeting and when the time came, he reduced me to a puddle in front of the ZD publishers and managers. He'd stop me and raise a question. "How many Impalas did Chevrolet sell last year?" When I turned to look it up in my Chevrolet Reference Guide, he stopped me. "You should know how many cars Chevvy sold for each and every model they make!" I answered almost meekly, "then I guess it follows that I should have that data for all of GM, Ford and Chrysler as well. We're talking thirty or forty models in all, Bill. Each with their own sales figures." He shrugged moving my response right off the table. "If you're setting yourself up as a know-it-all than you should have that data at your fingertips." Wow, again! I gave up. He eventually stopped which I took as a signal to get off that damned platform.

He'd then join me and walk to the other side of the room for privacy with his arm around my shoulder. "Who's the best salesman of every magazine staff at our company?" Id look at him and say, "Well it sure as hell isn't me, Bill. Not after that tear down."

Then he'd proceed to'tell me that I was not only the best but one of the few who could take criticism. I heard later that Ziff plowed into Dave Hartmann, a big guy built like a linebacker. Ziff brought Dave to tears during a discussion of the photography market. He probably asked Dave how many lenses Canon Camera sold that year.

*　*　*　*　*　*　*　*

Brad seemed to have trouble explaining himself, unusual for such an outstanding speaker. Ziff had just purchased Cycle Magazine from its owner in California. Tom Sergeant, a good friend, had been named publisher of Cycle about one week before. He was building a new sales staff. I began thinking about a new opportunity.

I was trying to digest what Brad had just said to me. He hadn't fired me. But he wasn't happy with me " continuing as publisher of Car and Driver." That had to mean he was firing me. If we had background music his words would nave been accompanied by the groan of a bass organ. He was slurring a word or two, talking as if trying to explain the    rational for my newfound dilemma. He sounded like he had a hockey puck stuck in his mouth. I interrupted him.

"You said you and Bill are 'dissatisfied'?"

"Well, yes."

For a man accustomed to addressing the highest levels of industry, I found his response banal, at best.

"I didn't even  hear a warning shot?" Brad.

"Mart, let's try not to make this any more difficult than it is."

"Can you give me a reason why you're firing me?"

Brad made mention of my not getting along with Hiufford and Hufford having his complaints. I thought using that hypothesis maybe Hufford should be the one to go.

He opened the folder – it documented my salary, pending commissions, bonuses, vacation balance, company car lease; stock membership in the Greenwich Country Club, and minutia of lesser import. This is final, I thought. Forget Cycle, Stereo Review and anything with the ZD logo on it. You are officially out of here, Martin Thomas. And Hufford has knifed you in the back.

We discussed the balance in my profit sharing fund, pending commissions, vacation days due and my company credit card. Two other perks from my position as publisher included membership in the Greenwich Country Club. I agreed that Ziff-Davis would be re-imbursed for the initiation fee in keeping with the Club's by-laws.

That left the company car that I assumed I'd return once it had been replaced. He asked me for the car keys without looking up. I was surprised and told him so.

"I thought since you've been terminated, you'd turn in the car, .as you have the Country Club membership, your credit card and the like." I started to steam. It was the first time I felt angry throughout this entire ordeal. I raised my voice. "Well, I'm not prepared to do that at this moment. I need the car to get home unless you insist. If you insist, I'll be happy to drive the car through the lobby, onto an elevator and drop it in your lap!" My upset with Briggs was accompanied by several violent curse words I will not use here. I surprised myself. I had raised my voice. People in the outer offices had to have heard me. Brad sat surprised. I didn't know whether he'd demand the car keys or not. If he did of course I had no intention of driving the car into the lobby. The car wouldn't fit in the elevator anyway.

He seemed to have cooled a bit as I did. "I think we're about finished here. Why don't you handle your other office details?" I turned on my heel before the girls came out of their offices and took a down elevator to the sixth floor.

My staff was scattered about. Most were wearing stone-like expressions. Not a smile in a carload, and why should there be? I felt uncomfortable. I forget my secretary's name. She advanced toward me and stopped; her nose almost touching mine. "What about me? Where am I supposed to go?" she asked in a loud voice. I told her I'd talk to her later.

I went to my office and sat at my desk. It occurred to me that I really had been fired less than one hour ago. I hadn't even time to draw a natural breath let alone handle personnel problems.

I opened the deep desk drawer on the left hand side of the desk and recalled placing a one-gallon bottle of Beefeater Gin in there several years ago. It was gone.

Ken Heath, one of my best salesmen, came by and asked if he could have my black leather couch.

I left before they could pick the rest of my bones. I called Maureen and confirmed my demise. I took another down elevator, which I thought appropriate. I walked out onto Park Avenue and there sat the prettiest site I had seen all day. Maureen sat in our silver BMW and I kissed her smile.

As soon as she dropped it into gear I realized we'd be driving north today but I had no idea where we'd be going tomorrow.

# Post-Mortem

## I resume breathing

It felt odd boarding the local at weird hour of 10:56 a.m. On a

Saturday morning no less. I didn't even know there was a local. I felt unemployed. Technically, I guess I was

I usually took the 7:32.express direct to Grand Central Station. It had a club car for Royalty. Overstuffed beautifully upholstered chairs on a swivel. Black waiters with white teeth and brass buttons served these Captains of the Universe with a "Mornin' Mistah Chairman." A hot cup of coffee in a china cup was served with the exact amount of sugar and/or cream, specifications placed with another attendant twenty years ago when these men bought their first club car ticket. I was just going to type captains of industry but I didn't think their manicured fingernails touched anything heavier than a stock quotation.

These men were chairmen of their Boards. They all lived in Greenwich. When Maureen and I moved into that stately town we told everyone the median income was going to plummet That was the commutation setting I was accustomed to for years.

Today was different. There were passengers on the 10:56 a.m.

who looked like they were without gainful employment. No suits, no ties and no jobs. Maybe today is a holiday, I thought. This was a whole new experience for me.

The husky young man sitting next to me was naked from the waist up. I glanced out of curiosity to see if he wore shoes but he was sitting on his feet.

No doubt some were avid Knickerbocker fans going to the

afternoon basketball game at Madison Square Garden. I was a Knicks fan, but never saw an afternoon anything and as I mentioned previously, never knew the train had a local. I was in my forties, the year was 1976 and the country's unemployment rate was probably insignificant. Why weren't these kids working? Once downtown it looked like half the City's high school kids were playing hookey.

I looked at my watch. If I was still employed I'd either be at lunch with a client or with my colleagues. The first drink of the day bathed the esophagus in wake-up call fashion – lunchtime! Maybe a second drink, maybe not, depending. Critical decisions when one has a job.

I wondered if my new deal, if I get one, would even come close to what I've had at ZD these past years. Probably be lucky to get a lunch hour. I was thinking negative. Don't wanna do that. Bad for hitting home runs, scoring touchdowns, getting a raise.

I walked from Grand Central smack into the oncoming lunch crowd too busy for anyone to notice anybody. I could have walked to ZD blindfolded. A temporary receptionist never stopped me. Good.

Brad was in his office. He asked how my 'lovely wife' took the events of yesterday. I told him she picked out some cruise wear with the profit sharing money for our trip around the world.

That would have been lies, all lies, mixed with a healthy dose of rage. Instead, I leveled with him. "She was too busy with the kids, Brad. There was no time to mention Detroit. Too important to do it in bits and pieces as I rushed to the train. It's best that I get the details first."

"Tell her she's going to be married to ZD's new Automotive Marketing Director. You'll start in Detroit and then go national. Cover the imports here in town before you have your west coast manager introduce you to the California car guys. You already know most of them from your Car and Driver work." Wow. It was sudden and it was impacted with heavy stuff. I had barely sat down. "Your income will be increased. You'll be the only one in any of our ZD offices with a company car so keep the one you still have."

Now there's a swtcheroo. Yesterday he asked for the car keys. Today, he practically said get it tuned up and hand us the bill. Something was wacky. Was Bill Ziff behind this? Did I have an angel in my corner?

Brad continued. "Pick out the country club of your choice. You'll be the only ZD employee with these perks same as you've always had here in New York." We certainly got off on the right foot.

"Brad, are you aware that I hired all those Car and Driver guys?

You're moving me into the same office. He took a moment to think about it. I guessed he might have overlooked that possibility. Finally, he spoke. "If they start to get to you just drive off in your company car and leave 'em in the dust." He was laughing at his own meager joke. I thought his attempt at humor equated with his inability to appear homeless.

He re-lit his pipe. If this were a movie, the director would insist Brad smoke his pipe in every scene, while wearing his Brooks Bros. tweeds.

The bowl of his pipe was packed tight, blue smoke drifted around the office as he spoke. "Oh, I almost forgot, Mart. We'll run full-page newspaper ads announcing your arrival in Detroit. Photos of you with explanatory copy on why you're moving to Detroit. Take a look at it before you leave. I don't think we've ever done that for anyone," he continued.

"Selling Psychology Today is a handful, as you probably know. The progress has been slow. You're going to change that. Bill and I feel the same way about your ability.

"I nave no concern that you won't be number one again." I wanted to ask him why he didn't feel that way when he fired me the day before. That would be poor judgment. Instead, a small voice inside me suggested I just let the air out of his tires.

It had been quite a couple of days. I went from post-mortem to getting an A+ in survival. I called Maureen and told her about the strong possibility of re-locating to Detroit. "Will you be home for dinner?" Judging from her cool response, I was going to have to make my first sales call sooner than planned.

# 24 Hrs. Later

### A reprieve?

This was Saturday morning. I heard the telephone ring but I didn't want to move my head. I felt recurring pinpoint explosions under my scalp. It's called the morning after you've been fired. .

Maureen picked up the receiver, turned the phone over to me and whispered, "it's Mr. Briggs." I tried to grab her left thigh for fun but she got away. First time in memory I ever missed. The kids all laughed.

"This is no time for hanky-panky!" she shrieked and then quickly covered her mouth. God forbid Mr. Briggs might suspect that we sleep together after five kids and twenty years, I joked. Briggs fired me yesterday morning.

Why is he calling me only twenty-four hours later? Ms. M. handed me the receiver.

"Hey, Mart! Sorry to call you on the weekend. Everything cool?"

Cool?" he asked. I snickered. Could've been the first time he used that word when he wasn't referring to the breeze across his deck in Connecticut. Brad was a WASP, forever faithful to the Old Boys' Club. Men who wear school ties, never use the word cool and hire only guys they went to school with.

He was nervous firing me yesterday. He seemed nervous today.

I thought I'd pull his leg. Rather than answer like a loyal soldier, after having been dishonorably discharged.

"Oh, sure, Brad. Why wouldn't everything be cool?

The family gathered around our piano while Anne Marie composed a funny little song -- "Daddy's Out Of Work." It's sung to "Three Blind Mice." We're getting requests from all over the neighborhood.

"I'm sorry, Mart. I wasn't thinking."

"I hope I didn't break any Ziff-Davis rules singing a smart-ass song even though I don't work there any more."

"Okay, Mart. You've made your point! You're upset and I'm not surprised. It hasn't even been twenty-four hours since we last met. I hope you've begun to settle down so we can talk." I wondered what he wanted to talk about. "Has the press called you?" I was stunned.

"The press? Why would they call me?"

"Have the N.Y. Times, Advertising Age, anyone in the ad press called you?" I was surprised he even entertained the idea. "Why would the press call me, Brad" He said he'd like me to keep my discharge quiet until we resolved a few things.

I decided to play the silent type and keep my mouth shut. Besides, I had already said too much.

"Mart, Bob Bonamee has left Psychology Today in Detroit for another magazine. I had no idea of this when we spoke yesterday. We didn't get word until first thing this morning, which is why I'm calling you so early today. As you know, Bob has been branch manager of Psych Today since we bought the magazine over a year ago.

"Bob's a died-in-the-wool golfer. He's joining Golf Digest. Now he'll probably be able to play seven days a week!"

I thought my friend Bob sure was lucky. I wished that I could inherit a deal like that with the right magazine.

"Golf Digest just had a an opening in Detroit and Bob's timing was perfect. He'll be leaving in two weeks"

"Good for him. I'll have to call him," I said.

"If you're interested in replacing Bob, and I certainly hope you are, I'd like you to listen to our offer. Don't react until you've spent time with Bill Ziff and me and thought about this opportunity plus everything that goes with it. "

It seemed like one big shunt. Re-locating to Detroit. Taking over a psycho magazine? Saving Ziff's ass in his time of need. But whose needs were being fulfilled?

"Can you get down here later today? I know it's short notice. We really don't have much time. Bill's leaving town this afternoon. I think you'll find it well worth your while"."

"You're talking me moving to Detroit, right?"

"That's one of the reasons why Bill and I took every facet into consideration. Can you get here by two o'clock?"

"I'll see you both at two," I said.

# GOLF POEMS

## Sunday, Bloody Sunday

I'm a Sunday morning warrior,
who frowns on golf's contrivance.
Like the club you hold, with its head of lead,
I pray no  members see us.

Is  your weapon made from moonstone, lad,
to impress your lady love?
Forget her! Instead  hit the fball,
and impress golf Gods above.

 Finish your  lifeless swing , (dear god!)
What is it that's  on your mind?
Your left leg points straight up in the air,
like a dog that sprays the pine.

You think that  you can play like me?
I practice daily on the range.
 Do you even know where it might be,
you'd best listen to this sage.

Be knowledgeable of every grain,
every blade that bars your ball,
avoid hazards like the plague, my boy,
then one day you will  enthrall.

When your ball  sails upward toward the sky
and you draw it, right to left.
Yes, you'll do this, in the bye and bye,
so  pelase don't feel bereft.

There'll be no hazards, on that special day,
all putts will roll into  the cup.
You'll stroll in victory from the 18th green
to the arms of your  buttercup!

marty toohey

## DOOMSVILLE

Pleas heard
'round the course

Hit a provisional
My shot just died.
I'm not getting distance
I keep slicing.

I keep hooking.
It didn't draw.
It didn't fade.

It never broke.
It broke too much.
I hit it thin.
I hit it fat.

I never hit it.
You peeked.
I'm gonna buy a10-wood.
I'm giving my wedge away.

His handicap's too high.
My handicap's too low.
They should make this a par 5.
They should make this a par 4.

Does he stroke here?
I was lined up wrong.
I pulled it.
I should stroke here.

I pushed it.
I stubbed it.
Shoulda taken a drop.

It's 90% air.
(and 100 % wood.)

I'm taking a lesson.
Mark it, or putt it.
You guys have lockjaw?
I've been using my old putter.

I bought a new wedge.
Never up, never in.
Slice!
Hook!

Alice!
The greens are fast.
The greens are slow.
I shoulda laid up.
I shoulda gone for it.

It's in the trap.
It's in the rough
It's in the water.

We takin' mulligans?
Shapiro's?
You dropped your shoulder.
You came over the top.


Bite!
Roll!
Turn!
Break!

Amen.

Trees

(With apologies to Joyce Kilmer)

I think that I shall always see,
Intimidation in a tree

A tree whose hungry mouth is pressed,
Against my golf ball, now a t rest.

A tree that looks at God all day,
Then tales my neat draw out of play.

A tree that shows it's summer wear,
Too many branches in her hair.

Upon whose bosom, snow has lain
Since course is closed, I must abstain.

Poems are made by fools like me,
the same such fools that hit a tree.

## Scores

They come and they go,
the scores we seek.
They'd be much lower,
if we didn't peek.

## Are We Having Fun Yet?

Of bogeys 'n doubles 'n triples 'n things
They happen to duffers and seniors and kings.
They are banes on our card, unsightly mars,
Which serve to move final scores, further from par.

What's perplexing is that there's no reason, nor rhyme
I've successfully parred these holes. No, not every time,
Wasn't it yesterday when I parred number 3?
But today, I hooked it right, now I'm sitting o.b.

I'm looking at a possible seven,
Making bogey would be like heaven.
Might my recalcitrance compound my fate?
Must be careful, or I'll score an eight!

TRUISMS

It matters not
the drive you got,
if you screweth up,
your second shot                    *
                                    *

Drive for show!
(but putt or dough.)
                                    *

The saddest words
of night or day,
Are those that say
"you're still away

## Tomorrow

In My Hand I Hold A Ball
White And Dimpled, Rather Small.
Oh, How Bland It Does Appear
This Harmless Looking Little Sphere.

By Its Size I Could Not Guess,
The Awesome Strength It Does Possess.
But Since I Fell Beneath Its Spell,
I've wandered through the Fires Of Hell.

My Life Has Not Been Quite The Same,
Since I Chose To Play This No-Brain Game.
It Rules My Mind For Hours On End,
A Fortune It Has Made Me Spend.

It Has Made Me Yell, Curse And Cry,
I Hate Myself And Want To Die.
It Promises A Thing Called Par,
If I Can Hit It Straight And Far.

To Master Such A Tiny Ball,
Should Not Be Very Hard At All.
But My Desires The Ball Refuses,
And Does Exactly As It Chooses.

It Hooks And Slices, Dribbles And Dies,
Even Disappears Before My Eyes.
Often It Will Have A Whim,
To Hit A Tree Or Take A Swim.

With Miles Of Grass On Which To Land,
It Finds A Tiny Patch Of Sand.
Then Has Me Offering Up My Soul.
If Only It Would Find The Hole.

It's Made Me Whimper Like A Pup,
And Swear That I Will Give It Up.
And Take To Drink To Ease My Sorrow,
But The Ball Knows I'll Be Back Tomorrow.

Author Unknown

## Trips

Memories of the sweet ones sometimes last forever. I was Detroit sales manager for Psychology Today and several college market magazines, Walter Joyce called.

Walter Joyce was promotion manager for himself, which is to say he was as independent as I was. He called me one night from San Francisco.

"Marty, I don't have much time so I'll be quick." Walter never has much time.

"Spit it out Walter. See if you can say it the first time." Walter stuttered. His close friends were allowed to kid him.

"I'll try. This could be good for you, providing you don't get too greedy."

"Was I too greedy the last time you called with that cock-a-mamey do-it-yourself magazine that we all thought was published by apes?"

"No. You weren't too greedy."

"Didn't they ask me to sign a contract for exactly what I wanted?"

"Yeah, yeah, yeah."

"Then why shouldn't I continue to be greedy?"

"OK, OK, Like I said, I'm on my way in to see Mr. Big." Walter hesitated. "He Owns Banana Republic. I forget his name."

"You forgot his name?"

"I'll remember it later. He's goanna ask me how much money you want."

"Give him a high number. We'll cut it back until we get what I want."

"This is no push-over. The guy owns Banana Republic."

Does he wear a pith helmet in public?"

"He wants to start a magazine based the fashions he carries. Yes, ice pith helmets, cargo pants with deep pockets for the Belgian Congo, and leather boots to go traipsing a across the Sahara."

"I think it makes for a romantic editorial story that will have the readers' heads dreaming about his clothing when I tell it," I said.

"Can you sell this magazine, Mart?"

"It's a natural, Walter. Picture me describing riding on the Orient Express with its secret agents, Siberian smugglers, and spies, especially the one sitting next to his girlfriend."

"Will he promise to do a feature on the Bronx?"

"The Bronx?"

"Yeah. I understand they're dressing like hunters these days and carry elephant guns even when they go shopping."

"Stop kliddin'."How much you want?"

"$2000 a month, guaranteed whether I sell any advertising or not."

"You're being greedy."

"And of course, at the usual 20%."

"You're one tuff s.o.b."

"Tell him it's worth it just to have me on the street."

"I'll call you back after I keep my appointment with what's-his-name."

\* \* \* \* \* \* \* \*

This was the sweet part of my business. If I wrote about the bitter parts, this book could double in size. Incidentally, I sold more ad pages than anyone on the staff. I did it again in the second issue with advertisers like Jeep running four-color spreads off the inside cover. GMC truck, Chevy Blazer and Ford's 4X4.

There's a bittersweet part to our story. The Banana Republic got sold to the Gap. The GAP CEO took one look at the magazine and almost ruptured himself.

"What in hell are we doing in the magazine business? Get rid of this!"

Our third issue had already gone to press. I was sales leader again. My Trips editor told me had a story planned for the fourth issue "Too bad. It's all about the Bronx, Mart. Did they carry elephant guns when you lived there?"

\* \* \* \* \* \* \* \*

P.S. Before we folded I got a handwritten note from the owner of Banana Republic. It said, "You're the first guy I ever gave a guarantee to. I'm glad I did." He signed it but I forget his name.

## The Games Of Summer

We owned the streets

Street cleaning water trucks
send remnants of children's
playthngs to toss and tumble
into memories of a bygone day.

Cherished recollections, stirred
by those who played
in yesteryear's joyful games.
The games of summer.

Broken playthings, once
discarded to watery graves,
begin swimming forever
in the currents of the mind.

Sissy's rusty skate key, tied
rollers to her shoes, but now
she's crying salty tears,
her dolly's dress got wet.

A dampened  matchbook cover
bares its wet and flaming kiss,
before a final hug, a last goodbye
to recall a life of bliss.

Crayola rides the  ripples,
ignores a scribbled note

"Don't forget the milk again"
Mom made bim take an oath.

Street cleaning water trucks
send remnants of children's
playthngs to toss and tumble
into memories of a bygone day.


Cherished recollections, stirred
by those who played
in yesteryear's joyful games.
The games of summer.


Broken playthings, once
discarded to watery graves,
begin swimming forever
in the currents of the mind.

Sissy's rusty skate key, tied
rollers to her shoes, but now
she's crying salty tears,
her dolly's dress got wet.

A damp matchbook cover
bares its wet and
flaming kiss, before a final

Crayola trxxxxxxxxxxxxxxxxxxxxxxxxxxxxxxxx
ignores an urgent, scribbled note

"bring home bread and milk".

A slice of rubber is all that's left,
of the ball we called Spaldeen.
Struck by Joey's awesome bat,
the greatest shot we've seen.

Morning's flowers, fragrances
of daffodils and lilacs blend
with curbs of stone and concrete,
to welcome a new day.

Cherished memories recalled
by those who played
in yesteryear's carefree games.
The games of summer.

A slice of rubber is all that's left,
of the ball we called Spaldeen.
Struck by Joey's awesome bat,
the greatest shot we've seen.

Morning's flowers, fragrances
of daffodils and lilacs blend
with curbs of stone and concrete,
to welcome a new day.

Cherished memories recalled
by those who played
in yesteryear's carefree games.
The games of summer.

## The Games Of Summer

Street cleaning water trucks
send remnants of yesteryear's
summer games,to swim forever
in the currents of the mind.

Broken playthings, once discarded,
toss and tumble in watery graves,
return as memories
of once upon a time.

Lizzie's rusty skate key,
tied rollers to her shoes,
now cries  salty tears,
her dolly 's dress got wet.

A  dampened  matchbook cover
bares its wet and pinked lips,
to brush Lizzie's cheek with a
flaming kiss, before a final dip.

Inside its moistened sheath,
a Crayola  swims upstream
toward  Connor's  note from Mother
to "bring home bread and milk".

A slice of rubber is all that's left,
of the ball we called Spaldeen.
Struck by Joey's awesome bat,
the greatest shot we've seen.

Water trucks wash remnants
of yesteryear's summer games
to swim forever
in the currents of the mind.

Tattered playthings, once discarded,
toss and tumble in watery graves,
shaping memories of an earlier time.

Johnny's wad of Double Bubble
casts its final imprint on
a flotsam stick of chalk, then
rides the raft of a baseball card.

A major league champion,
his many hits and runs,
lend promise to a boy with a bat,
and a ball and a glove.

Sissy's rusty skate key once
clamped rollers to her shoes.
She now sheds tears for a damaged doll,
whose party dress is wet.

Inside its moistned sheath,
a crayon, swims with Lizzie's
Brother's
shriveled note
to bring home bread and milk.

Our game cannot play without
the ball we called "Spaldeen",
struck by Joey's  bat today
the  greatest shot we've seen.

A dampened matchbook cover
bares its moist and pinked lips,
to brush Lizzie's cheek with a flaming kiss,
before a final dip.

Morning's flowers, fragrances,
of daffodils and lilacs soring
from curbs iof stone and comcrete
rife with tatttersall nd herbs.

From misty memories,
vapors rise  to celebrate
those who sang of  these joys.
The games of summer.

## Advices On (Poetic) Devices

My assonance is wearing thin
as metaphors fly by.
Alliterative shortcuts,
seem a wild and wooly ride.

Allusions come in sets of twins
relating two ideas.
The first one I don't understand,
the second could take years!

I may be lacking creative skills,
 (I sketched the horse before the cart).
Paintings that make sense to me,
are seldom called 'fine art'.

I used 'metonymy' one day
and substituted 'jerk'
For Mr. Chairman's rightful name,
He's known as 'Mr. Quirk'.

Most figurative languages
from poems tried and true,
do not come free and easily.
Might I be juxtaposed

# SAMMY

## June 18, 1913-January 15,1993

Sammy Cahn's lyrics brought hope to lovers everywhere.

When in doubt, he brought"High Hopes". Always forgave for, "Call Me Irresponsible. Support for "I've Heard That Song Before." With her till the final goodbye, "I'll Walk Alone". Reflection found the answer in, "I Fall In Love Too Easily". Together again," It's Magic" this time she begs, "Please Be Kind".

He told them love is a "Tender Trap" but both wanted" The Best of Everything". Some find it in "The Second Time Around" with a "Pocketful of Miracles" then dance in Chicago, "My Kind Of Town".

When "All That Love Went To Waste" they wanted to "Let Me Try Again". Sammy wrote for Frank, "Come Dance With Me", and she said yes. "Come Fly With Me," and she said yes, again. Precious moments," Day By Day," anxious pleas for "Five Minutes More" time to "Hang My Tears Out To Dry". Like clockwork, "Saturday Night Is The Loneliest Night Of The Week." He shrugs with indifference to "I Should Care", but deep down inside, "I Still Get Jealous".

Love overflows when, "It's Been A Long, Long Time, then roars like a blazing fire, "Let It Snow, Let It Snow". Soon, he'll pant for," Love And Marriage" as she begs, "Teach Me Tonight". He obliges, "Time After Time" as they recall memories of "The Things We Did Last Summer."

Thank you Sammy. Sleep warm.

# Big Band

## 52nd Street
## They called it Swing Street

This was 1948. I was already out of the Navy and barely twenty years old. The first time I ventured downtown to 52nd Street I bumped into Bobby Hackett, one of the greats. Any one could recognize Bobby's trumpet whether he played Dixieland, jazz or backed up of one of those Jackie Gleason lp's,"For Lovers Only". He was that good. We stood shoulder to shoulder, jammed at the Onyx Club bar, huddled inside a mass of music and the disciples of jazz, buffs all perfectly willing to engineer a body turn to accommodate a buddy's dry palate that way out of reach on the bar.

Clubs with entertainment had recently introduced something called a cover charge or a minimum. Customers like me and Johnny Linehan and whoever else was willing to take the subway downtown never sat at tables unless we were with a date and that by itself meant extra cash.

The sitters paid a premium for the table. We'd usually stand at the crowded bar in the front of the Club upon entering, which was really the back of the Club, if you follow me. We'd agree to buy the minimum two drinks. The result was an imbalance as the budget breakers viewed the show over the heads of "hoi piloi" or rich bitches as they cam to be known who acted as though they had a more acceptable birthright.

It didn't matter once the music started. When Stan Getz's saxophone blew the opening refrain to "I Can't Get Started", it was as if the entire congregation had turned to the same page in their hymnal and prayed together. I know I had experienced an epiphany.

Fifty Second Street regulars had heard the Stan Getz horn countless times probably standing in a similar barroom location. Hearing famous jazz musicians performing live in well known cabarets was all new to me but I caught on quickly. I was familiar with the big band stage shows at the Paramount Theater on Saturday mornings. But that was probably around the time most jazz musicians were going to bed.

The Onyx and the Three Deuces amd Jimmy Ryans, all Fifty Second Street clubs were very small inside. Performers walked in and out as though part of the audience. I had never been that close to the action before. Confident to some extent, I knew something of the music. I hoped that what my twenty years and boyish appearance lacked in self-esteem was offset by my sailor suit. It was 1948 and soldiers and sailors on leave still crowded Broadway and the Times Square areas.

They called fifty-second street "The Jazz Corner of the World" which didn't make sense since none of the clubs were located on the corner. But the label was as cool as the music. The Onyx Club and the others were in the middle of the block as close to each other as the musical notes that were to pour forth from the progressive bands led by Dizzy Gillespie who introduced something called bee-bop.

By 1948 I was out of the Navy but the earlier jazz inoculation would last forever. I traded in my uniform for what was called a zoot suit-- a 1948 craze created by jazz musicians. Trouser cuffs were pegged to hug the shoe tops and suit jackets lengthened to create the "zoot look".

The sales clerk at a store on Broadway called, "Brooks' Store of the Stars", told me that Billy Eckstine bought his oxford shirts that had a high collar. The collar flared as it framed the knot in his tie once it was buttoned-down. I knew that having seen Mr. B. perform.

"Mr. B. buys 'em by the box," he informed me. I bought one. It was white. I'd buy a second when payday rolled around. I did. It was pink, just like one of his.

I always ironed my oxford Brooks shirts to get that flared roll in the collar just like Billy Eckstine's. Once I heard him  sing from a postage stamp stage inside the Three Deuces. His hit record at the time, although he had several, was "I Apologize". When B leaned back on his six-foot slender frame and poured out the lyrics to that song white girls swooned the way they once did for Sinatra. Billy Eckstine had to be the best looking guy in the place, white or black. His features were Caucasian although his complexion was slightly dark. I guess the blue eyes settled it for the ladies.

They called him "Mr. B" and if you didn't think he was one of the best pop singers in the world you had to be tone deaf. Life Magazine put B's picture on the front cover that year and his records got as much radio play as Frank Sinatra. Rumor had it that the appearance of that issue of

Life caused problems in the South. Southerners didn't want daughters swooning over a black guy. But they did.

Musicians took breaks and sat on the fenders of parked cars outside the Clubs on The Street almost without notice. It was early in the musical cycle. The big bands were still holding forth. Bee-bop was still in its infancy.

Charlie Parker, dubbed "Bird", a complex man with a gargantuan appetitive for booze and food and women and later drugs. He eventually came to be known by a simple single syllable, "Bird", an irony in itself. "Bird" is all it took to Christen, establish and launch new Broadway club called Birdland. Dizzy Gillespie, Miles Davis and Lester Young took intermission breaks outside each club's entrance. They'd slouch against the fenders of parked cars, smoke cigarettes and talk to us.

Dizzy wore a beret and a tiny goatee just under his lip. You couldn't see it when he played trumpet. Told me it helped preserve his lip. Charlie "Yardbird" Parker, was a giant gentle man and smiled a lot while others made small talk about his music. I always felt Bird was preoccupied rearranging "Cherokee" on his tenor sax for the next set.

Lester Young, dubbed "The Prez" by Billie Holiday, wore a pork pie hat and an oversized black overcoat with sloping raglan sleeves that drooped almost as low as the smoky tones on his baritone horn.

I didn't realize who Miles Davis was or would become until later. He had a jet back complexion and wore deep dark shades that shut out the whites of his eyes. He appeared stoic much of the time and spoke in muted staccato fashion to other musicians that was kind of the way he played trumpet.

Billie Holiday, known as "Lady Day", sang at all the Clubs. She'd arrive in a taxi outside her club and always stop and talk to the musicians on break. Everyone called her Lady, as in Lady Day. She wore a large white gardenia on her dress each time she performed. I'd try to stand within earshot soaking up every sound. I wore out her recording of "Lover Man" and poured nickels into any juke box whenever it was listed on the title strips.

It must have been a payday when we'd decide to go downtown to the Deuces to hear Lady, amd later Sarah Vaughn, who blew everyone away with a voice that could travel three and lour octaves. I don't think Sassy ever made a bad record. She'd have a million-seller just reciting the Yellow Pages. Midway through one evening as we were still "nursing" our second beer, an entourage led a blind gentleman into the Club. He took his seat at the piano, a vibraphone, a bassist, and a drummer took their places. Within moments the announcer declared that we were about to hear from the George Shearing Quartet, recently having arrived from England and would we give t hem a big round of applause. What a treat!

I remember hearing, for the first time, what was to become an immediate Shearing hit - "September In The Rain" -- the song that became his theme. The crowd erupted with lasting applause and the group played several more songs. Soon he was led, as one would lead a blind man, through the Club, through the tables and past the bar where we stood. Another epiphany.

Only on Fifty Second Street

## Anita O'Day

### And Her Tears Flowed Like Wine

Anita O'Day's breathy voice and witty improvisations made her one of the most exciting jazz singers of the last century. Over five decades she suffered a nervous breakdown, a rape, numerous abortions, and a 14- year friendship with cocaine.

After short-lived stays as the girl singer with the top bands she went independent. Anita sang with almost every big band. She sang in small ballrooms, palm courts and quiet supper clubs.

Anita sang with Gene Krupa and Benny Goodman among among others. . When she recorded with Krupa and Goodman, she gave each band leader his first million-record seller; Krupa for "Let Me Off Uptown", with RoyEldridge, the first bi-racial recording ever made. She gained' nationwide attention on radio singing with Stan Kenton, where she recorded a novelty song, "And Her Tears Flowed Like Wine," which swept the country.

The disc gained record radio air play, and guaranteed bookings for any band that featured it in their play book. Anita recorded her last album at the age of 84, the same year she passed away.

## Woody

This was Monday morning. His Saturday morning big band show was great, as usual. Most of the energy and drive in the Woody Herman Band came from its leader. Woody was the epitome of 'hip'. Whether he was working with Ralph Burns on arranging "Early Autumn", the remarkably bluesy ballad copied by every big band; or sharing the loud, raucous and upbeat, big band sound of "Woodchoppers Ball", Woody Herman's fingerprints were all over his band's sound.

Woody's intellect and energy showed when leading the band with his piercing, high pitched clarinet, vocalizing its best selling ballads, or jumping to the beat of "Caledonia", the novelty song borrowed from Louis Jordan.

A gold satin banner, almost as long as the bus and two feet wide read, "The Woody Herman Herd". Underneath were the words, Appearing Tonight. Young musicians waited for his band bus to arrive so they could audition. Quitting the Herman band was tantamount to leaving Harvard. The big kids told us "the Herd is where they got their diploma."

This was Woody's Fourth Herd. He got up to seven Herds (before I lost track). His Second Herd featured a quartet of saxophones he called "The Four Brothers", featuring Dave Rickenburg, Jerry Pinter, Frank Tiberi and Mike Brignola.

Celebrated stars, members of the Herman Herd, like Stan Getz and Shorty Rodgers, played with the Bothers periodically.

"Blue Flame" was the band's theme song until 1939 when Woody had Ralph Burns wrote an arrangement that practically became the band's new theme song – it was called "Woodchoppers Ball", a sensation then, and still remembered today.

Burns, one of the top arrangers with Woody, had already penned "Early Autumn", the jazz classic. Like so many Woody Herman originals it had strong appeal for young musicians who studied the intricacies of his music of that day. In three years, "Early Autumn" sold five million copies, unheard of for those times.

Woody was "hip". His band played at the cutting edge of jazz and blues. New, abstract sounds with forced power, might best describe Woody's music.

All of his sidemen were outstanding examples of what made the Herman Herd sound unique.

When modern jazz, then called bee-bop, arrived on the music scene, most of Woody's peers rejected it. Tommy Dorsey once exclaimed, "They sound like they're practicing!"

Nonetheless, Woody asked Dizzy Gillespie, who was at the forefront of modern jazz, to write three arrangements for his band, something no other leader would ever do.

Woody played clarinet, alto sax and soprano sax. He was a vocalist with a broad range from ballads such as "Laura", a best-selling Woody Herman single, to novelty tunes like "Caledonia", another top-seller.

Outstanding jazz artists that played in the Herman band included the inimitable Fletcher Henderson who applied his post-graduate university studies to arrangements that comprised the Benny Goodman "playbook", the forerunner of what would be known as "swing".

Together with Don Redman, another outstanding arranger of the day, the two men fueled the exciting big band era that swept the nation into very facet of popular music lasting for decades.

Woody attracted musicians who would later become stars in their own right -- Zoot Sims, Al Cohn and Gene Ammonds. Later, Neil Hefti, award winning arranger and composer who came after Ralph Burns; Pete Condoli and the great Flip Philips, tenor sax. In the 1940's Chubby Jackson, master bass player, soloist and entertainer joined the band with great success.

Herman showcased many female vocalists, one of whom was Astrid Gilberto. Stan Getz and Astrid recorded the Brazilian favorite, "Girl From Ipanema" in 1963.

During his 64 years on the bandstand Herman changed the face of jazz and blues with fresh new arrangements he brought to the bandstand and his willingness to experiment.

## June Christy

Her voice poured like a mountain stream flowing onto a bleached stone stairway. June Christy was singing Midnight Sun. Her signature song stirred emotional memories for the overflow crowd inside Fifty Second Street's famed Onyx Club. Everyone ordered another drink.

This was in the 1950's and we were there. The song became a standard for Ms. Christy. It had gone topless without a lyric before then.

The instant Johnny Mercer heard the music on his car radio he dashed off the first seven lines using a pencil and a pad laying on the passenger's seat.

> Your lips were like a red and ruby chalice,
> warmer than the summer night.
> The clouds were like an alabaster palace,
> rising to a snowy height.
> Each star its own aurora borealis,
> suddenly you held me tight.
> I could see the midnight sun.
> Copyright Knopf Music Pub.

\*     \*     \*     \*     \*     \*     \*     \*

Rumor has it, during a songwriter's cocktail party back then, the perennial question, "Who is the greatest songwriter?" was raised again. Without hesitation one writer said, "I vote for Johnny," who was standing nearby.

"Any body who rhymed, ruby chalice, alabaster palace and aurora borealis gets my vote!"

# Big Band Themes

## Louis Armstrong

The moment the darkened stage gave way to a spot light's brilliance on Satchmo's familiar smile, you heard the first note of Sleepy Time Down South. From this single note through his entire performance there was no doubt that the man shaping this matchless sound through a trumpet was the man they called Satchmo.

For as long as he played, you knew there was no one else in this world that could make music sound as never before.

## Count Basie

Count Basie led his band of musicians through performances like a four-star general commanding a division of impeccably prepared troops on to ultimate victory.

He orchestrated a sound from sixteen or more musicians that sent crescendos of what big band was all about as high as the moon and as soft as his bell-like plinks on the high C notes at the far end of the keyboard.

## Charlie Barnet

In keeping with his heritage, Charlie Barnet introduced his band with Cherokee; an upbeat arrangement laced with tom-toms and saxophone solos that got dancers "out in the aisle" immediately.

Barnet led his middle-of--the-road orchestra throughout a career that offered a recognizable theme that was unmistakably Cherokee from the first note to the last.

## Glen Miller

The downbeat of Moonlight Serenade has filled dance floors with anxious "hep-cats" all over the world. The distinct combination of woodwind instruments that Miller concocted prompted everyone's desire to dance. The sound was evident not only in the theme but on the upbeat sound of Kalamazoo, Tuxedo Junction, In The Mood. It has been said that ships on the horizon recognized the Miller sound as it flowed from his brilliant woodwind arrangements to the ships at sea.

# SRI LANKA

## Preface

Sri Lanka clings to the southeastern corner of India like a teardrop on a cheek. This demoralized country has shed copious quantities of tears in defense of its once venerable civilization.

The first conflict occurred when a South Indian dynasty established its Tamil kingdom in Northern Sri Lanka during the sixth century. The Tami Tigers, as they came to be known, declared war on the Sinhalese, (Sri Lankans).

Tamis'military aim called for a quick and total conquest of the small country. Its goal was never realized nor did the Tami Tigers resolve ever waver. Declarations of war against Sri Lanka had the predictability of the seasons from that day forward.

In June of 2009, a small conflict kindled a large conflagration that Started And a full-blown war. Communications outlets closed, all media was stifled.

Source: Google

The story that follows is a fictionalized account of that war.

Sri Lanka has clung to the southeastern corner of India like a teardrop on a cheek. This demoralized country has shed copious tears in defense of its once venerable civilization. The first conflict occurred when a South Indian dynasty established a Tamil kingdom in Northern Sri Lanka during the sixth century. The Tami Tigers, as they came to be known , declared war on the Sinhalese, (Sri Lankans).

Tamis' military aim was fpr a quick and total conquest of the small country but its goal was never realized.

The Tami Tigers'resolve never wavered. Declarations of war against Sri Lanka had the predictability of the seasons. Three months ago, in June of this year,a small conflict kindled a major conflagration that initiated a full blown war.

Source: Google

The story that follows is a fictionalized account of that war.

\* \* \* \* \* \* \* \*

When the spring war was in its infancy, the Tami Tigers overwhelmed a regiment of the government's military in the central sector of Sri Lanka. The militants threatened the unarmed Sinhalese refugees with torture and death. Twenty-three Sri Lankan families were driven from their homes, schools and places of employment, as their ancestors were centuries ago.

Anskrit Nandakumar, became their appointed leader. He was a farmer in Columbo. The refugees continued to hurry in a direction away from where they estimated the militants had deployed.

Suddenly, all of the refugees came to a sudden stop. They called to Anskrit. They were horrified at the sight of human slaughter. Mothers shielded their children's eyes. Many turned away in revulsion. Another band of escapees had apparently attempted the same escape route earlier.

Body parts of more than one dozen bullet riddled bodies, some decapitated, lay strewn across their paths like misplaced oars. Bloodstained torsos were scattered in the path of the refugees who walked gingerly around the bodies, stepping over the body parts, holding even the children's hands. Further along the beach, refugees spotted the hull of an abandoned skiff, a boat that was set back from the water, Anskrit reached the boat and studied its size. He ordered the men to move the boat toward the water.

Several big men quickly volunteered and struggled to drag the heavy boat while Anskrit counted the number of refugees. Children can double-up, he told them. He looked about at the remnants of bodies lying all around them, then vowed with a silent prayer that no one would be left behind. They carried the boat out further into the water hoping their newly found craft was sea worthy.

Mothers, babies, grandparents, children of a young age, teens, cousins from extended families, and the men - -twenty-nine in all --were told to line up and climb into the boat, one at a time. One of he elderly women slipped on the wet deck of the boat but quickly received assistance. One had badly bruised her ankle but did not complain. The two men who waited behind had trouble moving the boat into the deeper water. With so many people on board, it was almost impossible. A third man, who was very tall, stepped from the boat and came to their aid. The boat moved and all three men climbed aboard as it slipped o--ut into the Indian Sea. While low in the water, it floated. There was some leakage but nothing unusual.

The tall man tried to start the outboard motor that coughed up a limp sputter at first, then died, as everyone's spirits sank. After a series of cranks the engine barely caught but kept sputtering. As the small engine's volume increased, it put a smile on everyone's face for the first time that day.

The boat started to move, slowly at first. The small engine Began to wheeze, then belch, then cough out loud, just like an old man clearing his throat. It struggled, but kept on humming. The tiny outboard was pulling a load that had to weigh more than two tons. Everyone felt that the engine was pulling its own weight, like a dedicated member of our ,group. We were on our way. It was finally time to relax. Before long, there were no sounds except for the awkward hum of the outboard motor. The silence was soothing.

After a while, most of the passengers tried to get some sleep. The menbegan to talk among themselves... . . . . . . ..

Why is everyone so quiet? We're out of danger.
And we'll soon be out of gasoline.
One is never out of danger living here.
Didn't our ancestors say the same thing?
What? Run out of gas?
No, you stupid! Run out of danger!

I heard my grandfather, after the last war, which incidentally was not the last war. When he was a young man and I was a little girl, he said, "Well, its over. Thank God. We can be normal people again." But it wasn't over. It never is. Less than one year later he passed away. And it started all over again. First a spark, then a fire, and then another war.

I was there, too. If you missed it, stick around. There's always another one behind it.Why doesn't any other country help us? The U.S. helps Kenya and Nairobi. They help Israel all the time.

What about Iraq?

You call that help? They spent 8 years there and a terrorist killed 15 with a bomb just last week.

Who spent 8 years in Iraq?

You forgot already? Don't let Bush hear you! 8 years in Iraq. The U.S. hasn't spent 8 minutes in Sri Lanka. You're talking ancient history. The U.S. left Iraq. Now they're in Afghanistan. Why couldn't they stop and say hello to us?

Maybe it's because they can't find us.
As someone said, we're like a teardrop about to evaporate. Forget Bush.
He's gone away to write his memoirs.
What's Obama going to do? Send more troops?
Send more troops? Don't these guys know that Russia tried that?
Russia pulled out.  So should the U.S.
Maybe we should ask the U.S. to visit?
By then †they'll probably be in Pakistan.
Do we have an ambassador?
Hey. Never mind about Ambassadors. Anyone bring food?
A woman joined the conversation for the first time. I brought bread and rolls.
Another woman spoke.
We brought it for the children.
What about water?
Anther woman spoke.
I poured every drop into my canvas bag. It's for the children.

*　　*　　*　　*　　*　　*　　*　　*

That's it, someone said.
And we don't have oars, someone else said.
Maybe we can we can float with the tide. Another one said.
It's a relief to be cool. We should wear a shirt tomorrow.
Everyone should try to get some sleep.
It's been a trying day for all of us.
And we're still trying.
Is that supposed to be funny?
How could it be funny if you said it first?

Don't fight gentlemen. There's not enough room in the boat.

Later that evening, the little engine that could, could no longer. The tiny motor gasped its final breath, taking with it the chugging sounds of hope. The course of the boat was now aimless. It floundered like a cork for the next four days. No food; very little water; a relentless sun beating down on blistered bodies; a formula for a slow death, but when? Then there are those who decide to die. They know when. Two men, on the brink of death, slipped over the side unannounced that evening.

Diarrhea began to set in. First one, then two refugees started to succumb to the unbearable conditions. Death arrived on board -- the elderly women who bruised her ankle boarding the boat earlier, stopped breathing. One of the men moved her to the stern. They planned to slip her into the water at an appropriate time. When all in the boat turned away, one of the women stood and recited a prayer to Buddha: "What better friend to have than Buddha, who changes the sorrows of your world into happiness?"

That evening, the refugees buried five more bodies. There was a five year-old girl who could no longer shed tears. The 3-yearold daughter of a woman named Jay Nityanjkana died in her mother's arms. M. Medusas lost his father first, followed by his sister, later his nephew, twin brothers and an uncle -- six in all.

A three-month-old baby girl, Nubian by name, survived because her mother breastfed her baby girl, almost day and night, from scorched, wilted, nipples.

On the fourth day he refugees reached land at a beach town called Indian Shores. They were almost too weak to recognize it. A limited staff from the nearby clinic rushed to the boat. Everyone needed assistance. The doctor and nurses began treating them for dehydration and medicated burned bodies.

The breastfeeding mother collapsed and died as the boat touched the shoreline. One of the rescue squad noticed Nubian lying alone on the deck while the others were being assisted from the boat. He gave the baby to a nurse in the clinic who placed the child in a baby crib for treatment.

The clinic at Indian Shores would serve as their home until Anskrit and two of the surviving men started to draw up a plan to return to Columbo. But first, everyone agreed, they would get much needed rest.

*   *   *   *   *   *   *   *

The sound of cannon fire nearby awakened everyone early the next morning. Shells were landing close by. The refugees were greeted by a regiment of Tami Tigers. The doctor, all of the nurses and the medical attendants were killed. The refugees were slaughtered.

*   *   *   *   *   *   *   *

On the following morning when it had been decided Indian Shores was safe for an official recounting of lives lost and records filed, one of the inspectors walked out of the clinic with an infant in his arms. "There appears to be one survivor. When she grows up and tells friends her life story, few will believe her.

## Minor Wounds

Fadil Dobraca's Croatian regiment was ordered to fall out and pitch campsites when it reached the town of Kupres on the outskirts of Bosnia.

The soldiers had advanced another ten miles through enemy territory, decimating small towns along their invasion path. Dobraca, an eighteen-year-old draftee, joined the regiment twenty-seven days ago. Not a day went by when he didn't hope to receive a major wound in order to gain official discharge from the Army.

He marched behind rows of bobbing helmets, the sound of heavy boots slogging in cadence through wet mud. After each battle, fewer soldiers returned to march. Relief came when the shrill from his first officer whistle pierced the air and brought the soldiers to a halt so the regiment could pitch campsites for the night.

Feeling intense pain from minor wounds suffered in earlier conflicts, Fadil Dobraca dragged his bleeding feet to the side of a bombed out road strewn with shattered debris from small wooden homes that once comprised a peaceful village. Neighboring gravesites clustered beneath crude markers on nearby hills. Charred branches of leafless trees that earlier served as green shade umbrellas during hot summer days now resembled a minefield of inverted swords.

Dobraca placed his assault rifle on a legless kitchen tabletop to keep it dry. He dragged a heavy wooden entrance door several meters to where it would cover the wet, soft mud and serve as a dry resting place to sleep that evening. Exhausted, he searched for the same dream of freedom that invaded his mind night after night since he first saw action. It was always identical to his dream of a previous night. He closed his eyes and the dream returned. He saw himself standing, once again, at the end of the same long line he had stood on in past dreams. The wooden sign he was familiar with pointed toward freedom. It hung directly over an official desk at the end of the long line. Fadil Dobraca stood rigid on his only leg and balanced himself on a crutch with his remaining arm. The stump from his war torn leg hung in silence and the empty sleeve of his ragged uniform flapped in the breeze.

Others on line wore civilian clothes, dry shoes, and heavy jackets. But Fadil Dobraca stood in a single mud caked boot, laces crusted with blood. He remembered fighting earlier in neighboring towns when he wore two boots until searing pieces of shrapnel from enemy artillery ripped an arm and a leg from his muscular torso causing major wounds that officially qualified him for discharge and freedom.

Dobraca blissfully whiled away the time under a brilliant blue sky as he did many times in previous dreams. The bright crisp air was foreign to cannon smoke. He looked about his surroundings anticipating periodic shellfire from heavy guns, but there was none. Those on line in front of him did not wear helmets that bobbed or boots that slogged through mud. Dobraca anticipated a peacetime job once he reached the officials desk. The long wait always allowed him time for peaceful reflection and a recounting of his good fortune.

"I am lucky that two shells found their targets and that I no longer suffer from only minor wounds because minor wounds do not merit official discharge," he murmured to himself.

"I could have suffered simple bullet wounds," he murmured to himself. "Only two chances out of hundreds are narrow odds. Luckily, I received two major wounds and both count officially." Others on line were oblivious to his presence.

"I might have suffered only simple bullet wounds on my body that could be quickly bandaged. Worse, the enemy fire could have missed me entirely and I would still be marching with both feet and two arms along with the others. Fadil Dobraca counted his blessings over and over every time he dreamed his dream.

"Losing only one arm and one leg," he thought, "still leaves me with one arm and one leg." He allowed a contented smile to conflict with the anguished features on his haggard, face.

"Two shells have set me free," he exclaimed to no one in particular. Fadil was confident that when he reached the freedom sign and spoke to the official he would be honorably discharged and receive a job. He had practiced his job interview every time he had his dream. "

My crutch will serve as my second leg and I need but one arm to work. I do not need two hands to operate a machine or to use a tool. It is good that the Army will officially discharge me as a soldier but I will not be dismissed as a worker for I can do almost any job."

Fadil Dobracas dream finally placed him in front of the officials desk, which sat under the freedom sign. As soon as the first question was asked of him a shrill from his officer's whistle shattered Fadil Doric's dream waking him to attention. He forced his bloody feet into mud caked boots, picked up his assault rifle and began to march with others who suffered only minor wounds.

## The sounds of War

Where is the sound of he melon man?

The sounds in his streets were torn from the fabric of his life—a reflection of who he was, how he lived.

Iraq changed all that.

No longer would he hear those familiar street sounds. No peddler's singsong chants on the streets of Karkuk or Baghdad. NOt a sound from any fruit and vegetable peddler riding in his horse-drawn wagon as he remembered the clickety-clock over Fulton Avenue's cobble stones. No celebratton of produce, proclaiming—reddd ripe to-ma-tooos-hhs, beeg deelicious sqv-ash -- his speech accented in Russian that everyone's mother understood.

Those sounds were gone.

Instead, as a soldier, he heard prayerful benedictions

In strange language repeaedly, over and over amd then again. Could man be so unworthy he must beg forgiveness again and again, all day long, and again tomorrow hoping to purify his soul?

Do sinners in prayerful dedication beneath covered heads, masked faces and bodies cloaked against the seasons, also terrorize an outside world? He thought of his produce man who always sat unshaven, but not bearded, beneath a weathered cap. He would sing the praises of the largest squash in his wagon or suggest the joo-seymeloan Ripe joosey meloanes" fortified with a language garnished in accents of the old country spice.

He recalled the sound of the vendor's throaty voice prompting a final note that danced to its next destination. The gasping note reminded him of a banshee in mid-air for as long as the peddler's nicoteined lungs allowed.

The day he arrived to search for an enemy called al-Qaeda, who had left, but to where? Only sounds of war, the load and lock of rifles prepped to kill; unfamiliar sounds of crushed stone flattened under oversized truck tires that support massive military vehicles – troop carriers- taking moe and more soldiers into battle to replace those who were there but are there no more.

Crossfire bullets brought diverse sounds—a single flurry of automatic bursts, then detonation from explosions disguised as common walkways. A modern device althugh hand-made tloday by illiterate hands. They're called I.E.D's (independent electric devices). Set to deceive those who challenged with life and limb.

It was then he heard the sounds of the streets, Iraq streets, Hillah and later that same day, the sounds of more Itaq streets in Samarra, where Taliban live and work and kill. Different sounds.

An unbearable sound of war muffled those sounds. Ice cream pops, vanilla cones, popsicles and Italian ices, once brought the sound of children, but there is no room for ice cream, there are no children, but always room for more guns, more troops.

How does one sleep without the nighttime bangs and booms of garbage truck's advancing roar? Where is the lonely sound of the elevated train's midnight thunp-dee-dum, thump-dee-dum—a metronome for the sleep-deprived.

Soldiers must trade the joyful sounds of peace for the defeating sounds of war and wait.. …for the sounds of silence.

## Bill

He shot, but he missed Bill had an unusual characteristic for a cop. He was a loner – didn't have a friend in the world, as far as we knew and we were fourteen and fifteen years of age.

Bill was a New York City policeman. The big guys on the block hung out at Pop Beekman's candy store. It was during World War II. They were waiting to be drafted into the Army.

Bill was almost their age. Yet, he ignored the big guys whenever he passed them on his way in or out of Pop Beekman's. That's where he always bought cigarettes and a newspaper but never mixed with the older guys, the 17 and 18 year olds.

He was only a couple years older yet he'd pass them right by each time he went in or out of Beekman's without stopping to say hello. We knew the big guys  - Tom Meany, Ftats Frasso, Artie Beck, Joey Schaentzler-- they told us Bill walked past them every day without saying "hi".

One day, six of us kids were playing curb ball on Franklin Avenue. Curb ball was a nothing kind of game that we played until we got serious and decided to play choose-up stickball, or walk across town to the sandlot and play real baseball at Kingsbridge Park.

On this day, Bill seemed to appear out of nowhere. He waved in our direction even though we didn't wave at him. He stopped to watch us, even came across the street and made himself part of our game.  He laughed when we laughed; he shouted when one of us was "safe" or "out" like he was the umpire or something. We weren't even keeping score --just fooling around. He stood in the way of our game but none of us wanted to say anything to him so we moved.  He broke the momentary silence by offering to buy us a Pepsi.

"How many of you guys would like to come up to my place for a cold drink?' No one answered. "Come on, fellas. I'm buying. the drinks!"

He walked toward Jackie, my cousin, and wrapped his  arm around Jackie's shoulder in a friendly way, walking away from the game pulling Jackie with him. "Hey. Isn't anyone thirsty? It's a hot summer day! Come on. I won't bite you," he snickered. We began to straggle slowly in his direction while buzzing to each other. "

"You wanna go?" "What the heck, we're all together." "We'll get a free Pepsi."

Boff Barrett, the biggest amongst us, in fact the biggest kid in our class, addressed him. "It's a nice offer, mister. But we don't even know who you are."

"Well, that's the whole idea. What's your name, buddy?" Boff told him his name. "That's the whole idea, Boff. I just wanna get to klnow the people in my new neighborhood. I thought I'd start with you guys. Maybe have a Pepsi and get to know each other." Some of us wanted to suggest he get to know the big guys but no one had the nerve to say it.

We began to walk slowly as a group with Bill leading the way. Jackie got out from under Bill's arm so he could walk with us.

Bill just rambled the whole way to his apartment, which didn't' take very long. Everyone kind of felt it was okay to go. He talked about where he used to live, why he joined the police department, and bits and pieces of rhetoric that none of us really cared about.

His apartment looked okay. Nothing special. There was a display of firearms - various types of pistols - on the wall over the fireplace. It was really neat. The guns were different shapes and sizes. One especially looked neat. It had a white pearl handle.

He told us to sit down and to "make yourselves comfortable". So we did. He called from the kitchen. "You guys want a glass or drink it from the bottle?" There were just a few smothered grunts from us that revealed nothing.

"I like lotsa ice," JP finally called out. "Me too!" said Jimmy Mazy. They were the only intelligible words spoken since we met him. He carried in six bottles of Pepsi, two glasses filled with ice and a bowl of Cheeze-Its. "Help yourself, guys. I'm gonna have me a real drink."

He opened what looked like a liquor cabinet since there was quite a selection of bottles on the lower shelf. "I think a nice cold gin and tonic would be perfect on this summer afternoon. I got anything anyone wants - whiskey, scotch, rum - anything. I treat my guests like royalty when we party." He opened a bottle of gin that had already been opened, and a bottle of tonic.

"I guess you guys know, or maybe you don't, that most cops have a reputation for heavy boozin'. I'm not defending it. I just don't think it's anybody's business." He seemed to be apologizing and he hadn't even taken his first sip. I don't know if you guys understand. Cops are under stress almost every minute we're on the job, never knowing what's going to happen next. A drink now and then helps calm the nerves and keeps that trigger finger steady." He pointed to one of the pistols. What he said about the trigger finger sounded weird. Sometimes my trigger finger gets itchy," he said. We didn't know what he meant by that.

"You ever shoot anybody?" asked Boff.

"Only once, Boff. He was getting away from a grocery store robbery and I shot him in the back of his neck. "

"Didja kill him?"

"I think he recovered in the hospital. If he did, and I never bothered to check on the s.o.b. but I'm certain he's in prison."

"Would any of you like to see some of these guns?" he asked.

Several of us nodded since we all really wanted to see them up close.

"If you're good, I may even let you hold one, but no shooting!" he joked.

"I love guns," he said draining his drink. "I'm a collector. Some people collect antiques, or old jewelry, lotsa things. I collect pistols and some of them are 'antique collector' rated. Some of them go way back as you'll soon see."

He reached up to the gun display. "Hey, Boff, can you give me a hand taking this down? It's a little unwieldy." As Boff came across the room to help, Bill made himself another drink, tasted it, smacked his lips and turned back to Boff. He took hold of the other side of the gun display "It's not heavy at all, just a little unwieldy," said Bill, for the second time. They laid the display on a dining room able. The oak carvings in the woodwork around the frame were really impressive and looked real. Bright solid brass couplings fastened each of the pistols in place. It looked like it was in a museum.

"You're in for a real treat," he said. He held one pistol up as he began showing them. "Here's one called the Browning .19 mm. it's an automatic pistol." Pete Meehan said it looked like Dick Tracey's pistol in the comic strip, and it did. "That's because when an artist, especially a comic book artist, has to include a pistol in his drawing, he usually selects one that looks like a Browning because Brownings look like a gun. There are other pistols that are almost works of art, and I have some, but they don't look as rugged." He passed the Browning around and we each held it. Everyone agreed it was quite heavy to hold.

"You've all heard of the Derringer, maybe even seen it used in foreign films, where the bad guy, usually played by Peter Lorre or some other creep, had to conceal it from view. That's one of the advantages of the Derringer. You can hide it easily.

He placed the Derringer back in place and released another pistol. This is called a Revolver. When this pistol was introduced, it immediately sold out all over the world. It feeds bullets, delivering multiple loads, into one barrel in quick succession. Soldiers, and bandits no longer needed the time to re-load.

"Here's a German Lugar most recognize. I'm sure you all heard about it or saw it in those war movies with the Nazi officers brandishing their German lugers, kept in those large leather holsters, and worn high on heir hip.

"There are many different kinds of automatics, too many to discuss today. Finally, this is the famous Colt .45, used by the U.S. Army starting in 1909. Everyman's favorite. You've seen dozens of movies from that era - mostly John Wayne flicks- like, "She Wore A Yellow Ribbon." All the Hollywood movie studios keep a constant supply of Colt .45's for their westerns. I use the Colt all the time when I go shooting at the local target range. If anyone knows where it is in this part of town lemmee know. I have to stay sharp for when I'm on duty. I practice every Sunday," he said.

"Lemmee pour myself another drink." He filled his glass to the brim and drank half of it in one gulp without adding any tonic. Then he turned back to the gun display almost losing his balance. "How abut the rest of you? Anyone want more soda?" Well, I'd offer you some of what I'm drinkin' if you were old enough. But don't worry, I won't tell!" he said, now smiling, but in a strange way.

Bill picked up a revolver and started spinning it around his finger like the cowboys in the movies do. We were impressed. Boff said, "Hey, not bad!" Bill said, "You ain't seen nothing yet!" and kept twirling. He put on a small show for us on how to flip the pistol one way, then the other, spinning along the way.

"Lemme go get my hat. I'll show you guys what I look like when I'm the sheriff and I ride the trails."

I used the break to go to the rest room. I returned just as he came back from the bedroom wearing a white cowboy hat and brandishing a different pistol. He appeared to be very serious. He had assumed the stance of someone who was about to fire his pistol -- knees slightly bent and his pistol was now pointing directly at me.

He had a wild look in his eyes as he took one step toward me and slapped me across the face. It really stung but I acted like it was nothing. "Don't you ever stand in front of a loaded gun!" he yelled. I must have turned white. All the guys looked surprised and scared. H repeated his order. "Don't stand in front of a gun, whether it's loaded or not! Hear me?" Wow, I thought. He wasn't kidding.

I tried to say, "I didn't see you coming, or I didn't think it was loaded," but he stepped on all over my words with his booming voice. .

"How did you know this gun wasn't loaded?" he asked. "You got some kind of mental telepathy or something?" He stuck his face right up against mine. I could smell the booze. I tried to hold my breath and walked away, really scared. We were suddenly dealing with a guy and a gun and both were loaded. He was laughing, almost normally now. "Bet you'll never walk in front of a gun again," he said right in my face.

With that he turned and fired a bullet into the fireplace. It ricocheted off the stone and flew back toward him. Everyone must have jumped four feet! What a noise it made!

"See? You can never tell when a gun is loaded so you never point it at anyone. And you certainly don't walk in front of it," he said, again looking at me.

"I'm way ahead of you guys. What's wrong? Don't like my hospitality? Well wait'll you see what I've got to show you, now!" He turned on his heel, went back to his bedroom and seemed to forget the incident. Some of the guys suggested we leave.

"Wait'll you see my masterpiece!" he shouted from inside his bedroom. "I keep it on the top shelf in case I get robbed."

While he was gone Johnnie Grant and Petey suggested we leave. "I think we're overdue," said Boff. I agreed. We all stood up, while calling out a goodbye to Bill, thinking we were finally leaving.

He returned, wearing his holster, wearing his cowboy hat. and wearing a hostile look on his face. "Nobody's going anywhere!" he said. He motioned with his pistol directly at us for us to return to our seats. "Your young friend over there," he said, pointing to me again, "said he wasn't sure my gun was loaded. Well, there can be no doubt about it this time."

"Let's see if this pistol is loaded. As if I didn't know," he said, with that silly look on his face. "Everybody stand still!" he ordered.

"Don't move or I'll shoot!" How many times have you heard that in the movies.? Well, I won't shoot you if you move." Then he added, " just don't move too far," he said, laughing out loud.

He pointed to his holster. "This holster was passed down to me by my Grandpappy, who they tell me shot his share of Indians living out on the plains. Gave it to me when he learned I wanted too become a cop." The holster looked like a classic of some kind, all hand-carved with leather tassels hanging from it. He started twirling the pistol; again shifting it from one hand to another, passing the pistol into his holster, than taking it out as though he was aiming at someone." He was really practiced but we were too scared to enjoy it.

"Lemmee go get my boots. Can't go shootin' if you're not wearing boots," he said.

Boff turned and looked at each of us, motioning toward the door. We all got the message. He whispered, "Wait'll he's inside"

We waited a moment, giving Bill time to get as far inside as possible. When Boff was ready, he quietly said, "Go! Now!" We all took off. Three of us almost squeezed through the hallway door opening at the same time. The six of us flew down three flights of stairs hardly touching the steps.

"I think we better keep running," said Boff, "just in case he follows us." Suddenly, we heard a gun shot. It sounded like a loud clap of thunder.

The marble hallway must have caused the sound to reverberate. Then there was another shot. Boom!

The sound was getting closer. "He must be coming down the stairs," said Johnnie.

We ran up the hill to Beekman's and met up with the big guys. We were all out of breath. We told them about our experience most of us talking at the same time. Fat Frasso held his hands up to quiet us down. "Stop. Slow down. You say this guy is coming after you with a gun?" We all started again to answer at the same time, again. "He shot his gun twice inside his house!" we told them. "And twice in the hallway," said Jim Mazy.

Fat looked down the block toward Bill's apartment building. "I don't see anyone leaving his house. But all six of you can't be making up a story like this. "What do you think, Boff?"

"That's the way it was, Fats," said Boff.

"I'm gonna call the cops!" said Fats, and he did. In the meantime we could hear the neighbors screaming. He must be coming down the stairs at them.

"He's going to kill all of is!" said Mrs. Dworkind. "And my husband isn't here!"

Two other ladies started screaming as he kept firing his pistol. A crowd began to gather. Two police cars stopped and told everyone to stand back. They pulled their pistols and went into the hallway. We heard another shot. Then we saw Bill being taken in handcuffs to the police car. An ambulance came for the ladies.

"Boy! Were we excited!

"It's a good thing you guys told us," said Tom Meaney. "He would have gotten away if it wasn't for you guys. So I guess you can say you guys.

Every time we tell our story, we add, "Because of us, he was sentenced to prison for twenty years." Twenty years? How come so long?", they'd ask. We'd say," Because we were the witnesses at his trial and we told it like it is."

# TIME FOR A CHANGE

## Buy the Porsche

At first, the thought of having a vasectomy gave me concern. However, the alternative seemed worse. My wife, Maureen, would have to have her tubes tied, a painful process in the late 1960's. We already had five children. A vasectomy appeared to be a logical answer.

A news story that publicized Bing Crosby's new family appeared in the newspaper around that time. Bing had married for the second time, several years back, and the story carried photographs of his second family, now fully grown. He had five children with his first wife before she passed away. His second marriage brought about two additional children.

I had five children with my first wife. Suppose, God forbid, Maureen passed away, and I remarried. A long shot, but suppose it happened and my second wife wanted children. What then?

If Bing Crosby didn't opt for a vasectomy, due to personal preference or perhaps religious reasons, who am I to do otherwise? The Bing story gave me reasons to re-consider. I visualized talking with Bing in a scene from "Going My Way," where he not only played an understanding priest but also had most of the country feel that he could have made one helluva Pope.

ME: Father Bing, what do you think about vasectomy.

BING: (in his dulcet tones) Well young man, I don't think anyone should mess with what the good Lord has in store for us. Who is to say how many children are too many? You? Me? (he hesitated in dramatic fashion and lit his pipe). Or the man upstairs?

Jeez! Father Bing was no help. Now I felt like I was challenging everything I believed in since I was six years old. My indecision was taking on a life of its own. Next thing you know I might even become a Protestant. Instead of going to St. Cecilia's, I'd have the family going to that big Protestant church on the corner that we knew nothing about.

How would the kids feel about the move? I may as well take them out of parochial school. No more statues of the Saints and the Blessed Virgin inside the Church. Someone told me that Protestants don't do saints. No more crosses with Jesus hanging on the classroom walls.

How would my daughters explain this change in their lives to Sister Eileen, their beloved school Principal? I didn't have a vasectomy problem; I had a change of life problem. I was considering becoming someone else. I was becoming a modern day Martin Luther!

After a decent night's sleep, I decided with a clear head, plans for that day. We'd drive down to Manhattan from our Englewood, New Jersey home, and ask for a command performance by Francis Cardinal Spellman, no less. May as well go all the way to the top. His residence was on Madison Avenue. We'd take all five kids. Tim would ride in the stroller. I'd carry Terrence, Anne Marie, Christine, and Patty would walk with their mother.

I'd ask for a hearing. I would not mention the word vasectomy for fear that the Cardinal's hallowed walls might come tumbling down. I'd simply ask permission to practice another form of birth control. I'd get to the specifics, later. Maureen liked my plan.

We found a parking space on Fifty-second Street just two blocks away. We all marched across Madison Avenue to the Cardinal's residence. Maureen stayed with the five kids in the outside foyer and I met with the receptionist.

"May I help you, sir?

"My wife and I would like a meeting with the Cardinal."

"The Cardinal is not available today. What is it you wanted to see him about?"

"I would like to discuss the teachings of the Church."

"Which teachings might they be, sir?"

"Just one in particular, but I'd rather wait until I gain a hearing."

"The Cardinal is quite busy as I'm sure you can appreciate. He does have a staff on hand to handle such requests. Would you like to see Father Murphy? He is here today and I'm certain he will make time for you." I figured the alternative would be better than waiting until the Cardinal had an opening in his schedule.

"Allow me to bring my family in. I'd like my wife to attend the meeting." We filled Father Murphy's office.

The priest reared back in his chair with surprise when our family filed into his office. He appeared to be quite tall but did not stand up when we entered. Father Murphy was beyond middle age and then some. His demeanor was stern, his face apple red.

"What can I do for you?" he asked in a gruff voice. I thought if I answered that question truthfully, the Cardinal's residence and all of Rome would experience a colossal earthquake.

"This is my wife, and these are our children, Father. We have enjoyed nine years of marriage and have given birth to five children, six actually, but we lost one two years ago at birth. We practice birth control – the 'rhythm method', as approved by the Church. Our batting average is nothing to cheer about. At this rate we'll soon qualify for a license to run a day care center." I thought Bing Crosby might have laughed. Father Murphy didn't even crack a smile.

"Oh, I see where you're going with this. I thought so when you walked all of your children into my office. I can save both of us a lot of time by quoting the Pope's Encyclical on birth control that you probably already have read. Nothing can change that. There are no exceptions to this Papal ruling whether you have five or ten or more children. So I'll save both of us a lot of time and end this conversation for there can be no questioning a Pope's encyclical." We listened to Father Murphy for a few more minutes but the die had been cast. Vasectomy was a no-no.

My wife and I discussed the meeting on the drive back home, for what it was worth, and decided that I would enter Columbian Presbyterian Hospital at the earliest opportunity and have the vasectomy performed. There would be no other radical changes in our lives certainly not in regards to our religious lifestyle. We'd still attend Sunday Mass and the kids would still have statues in their classrooms. We would not become Protestants. I scheduled an appointment for surgery the following week at Columbian Presbyterian Hospital.

I was the sales manager of Car and Driver at the time. The surgeon apparently learned of this before I climbed aboard his operating table. All he wanted to do was talk about the new model cars. I think he said he had driven Jaguars for ten years. My mind was one thousand miles away. As he applied his sharpened scalpel to my private parts, he continued to compare various cars, trying to decide which one to buy. I lay in a vulnerable position wondering just how sharp his scalpel was – had he ever slipped?

His nurse assisted in the procedure. When she wasn't talking to the surgeon about the party she attended the night before, she just stared at my privates and reassured me that everything was going along just fine. She kept calling me honey. I had taken the bus over the bridge to the hospital. How did I get here, I wondered? Did I get off at the proper bus stop? Was I in the back of a garage having all this done illegally?

I was shocked that the surgeon would find this emotionally frantic moment to ask me directly, which was the best car to buy.

"Has your magazine road tested all of the cars for the new model year?"

I barely mumbled something incoherent. He didn't notice.

"I've been a Jaguar fan for years but I'm leaning toward buying a new Porsche. Whadda you think?"

I could feel beads of perspiration on my forehead. My body was fraught with anxiety. I heard what I hoped was the surgeon's scalpel snip the final snip. A moment later I heard him say, "Mission accomplished. You're a new man."

My first inclination was to touch my privates to see if they were still there. All I felt was hospital dressing followed by more hospital dressing. I wondered if I could get my pants back on over the bandages. Would I be able to zip up?

The nurse leaned over me. "So how do you feel, honey?"

"Not all that bad. A little dopey." Then the surgeon joined in.

"So whadda ya think?"

"Feels okay," I said. "But let's see if it works."

"I'm talking about cars," he said.

"I'm talking about kids. So I can no longer have kids?" I asked.

"No more kids," he said.

I took a moment to think about what that meant. It seemed so final. My head finally cleared. I addressed the surgeon.

"How long you been driving Jaguars?" I asked.

"Ten years."

"Buy the Porsche. It's time for

# My Landlady

## Windows are accessories?

Our divorce was final. It wa quite a while ago.We were close to finishing the division of property. I felt my ex-partner had used long division theories on me that were unknown even at the U.S. Treasury and convicted counterfeiters.

I sensed an argument coming from Maureen, my ex. She stood pointing to an oil painting I was holding. "Are you sure you didn't give that to me for an anniversary gift? I remember hanging it in one of our kids' rooms

"No, you're hallucinating again. I hung it in my office cause you gave it to me," I said. "You did hang the other thirteen paintings I gave you. If things ever get slow for you, which is highly doubtful, you can always open an art gallery."

My ex snickered and continued. "Are you taking the Steuben?"

Glassfish? I always liked that," she said." "The gill," I said, "on the fish's right side, has been broken off. I guess that's why I'm getting it." She picked it up and checked the gill. Satisfied, she put it back with my share..

"You always positioned it facing a wall." I placed it on the bottom of my garbage bag. .

"I hope my new condo has a wall," I said. I thought I was being funny. No one laughed except our son, Tim. I could make Tim laugh at a hanging ceremony.

Our property had been, not sub-divided—re-divided, so many times my ex had the lion's share of everything, lots of jewelry and arty things. I had lots of shirts and ties.

"You could never decide what you wanted so I'd buy you another shirt and tie." I wondered if I'd see a trash barrel on the way to my car.

A plastic garbage bag held my wine bottle opener; my high school yearbook with the word love scrawled on a page inside. Her name was Lizzy McCabe. She had blazing red hair. I took her to the movies when we were fifteen. I forget who paid. We sat in the second balcony and kissed.

It was my turn to hallucinate. I imagined Lizzie would come crashing through our glass patio doors any moment, and carry me away in her Lamborghini. I wondered if she could still walk.

There was a sleeve of golf balls in the bottom of the garbage bag I found in the kitchen sink. It smelled. It held a roll of sticky-tape for the handle of my tennis racket; the tape had stuck to a large glass ashtray. Rolls of foreign coins from Britain, Sweden and Spain, probably worth a few kroners or I wouldn't have carried them all the way from Europe.

I hid my golf clubs in the trunk of my car one week before. I know it sounds strange but I was concerned that she'd take lessons that week, discover the glories of the game of golf—and take off with my clubs.

I owned the first issue of Sports Illustrated, dated August 16, 1954. The magazine once had a value of $150 to $200. Maureen kept eyeing it. "I'll trade you my magazine for ten of your gold bracelets," I said, just kidding. But once again, no one laughed. I wondered if she had traded my sense of humor for a small-framed picture of her relatives whom she despised.

I packed my stuff in the garbage bag and held onto the rolls of foreign coins. I thought Id pay for dinner with them just to watch the waiter try to figure my tab. I offered him fifteen percent but he must have thought, "fifteen percent of what?I drove fast and watched for a stray Lamborghini. I was late for my appointment with my intended landlady whose name was Grace Yu. She was Chinese. Grace Yu owned six condos, side by side, facing Brown Street in Birmingham. Great location. She walked me to the empty unit.

It was small but clean. Had an outside deck. Grace began to outline the benefits I'd enjoy as a tenant in her condo—an outside upper deck, large screen TV, weekly trash removal, a fresh paint job, and a grocery store across the street that a lady friend told me was where she buys her imported beer. "I'll come over with a few bottles once you get settled. Lemmee know." I was all for cracking one open like now. She could be my very first guest. She said she'd settle for second.

Grace Yu's perk list soon included windows, the stove, refrig, and the kitchen cabinets. I stopped her. "Grace, you forgot to include fresh air and floors." And walls, depending, I thought.

She looked stunned. Have a/c on wall. You turn up." That's not what I meant. Water and floors are standard everywhere." Grace shook her head. "No standard in China," she said, with a cute little smile.

Grace talked with machine-gun rapidity. I thought it sounded like a kind of broken Chinese but what did I know? I learned that questioning Grace's speech pattern was a moot exercise.

I located the telephone number of a young lady whom I had known from an adult education class. We drifted away some time ago. I probably screwed up that relationship, too. She said she was surprised to hear my voice again. She agreed to meet me for coffee in Archie's, a coffee house on the Wayne State campus. Anna Mae Wong was the name I always called her. She loved it. She always signed her small notes to me that way. The notes often took the place of dates. I competed with a class schedule that must have been programmed in a labor camp.

Anna Mae was studying for her PhD. in the sciences. The moment I saw her I wanted to run for President and name Anna Mae in charge of all things nuclear.

In addition to her cultured brain, a considerable portion of her beautiful body, Anna Mae wore a blush cosmetic with a paper-thin cream; she had proud breasts; shapely legs by God that must cause atheists to re-consider. She stood opposite me like a porcelain sculpture; the toes of her stiletto heels angled in just a touch. Anna Mae wore brief short-shorts that made nudity appear to be so yesterday. Her jet-black hair, in the opinion of au courant wig makers, would pay a Warlord's ransom.

After we compared notes on our respective lives since last seeing each other, Anna spoke. She told me Grace's broken Chinese was a ploy.

"Some use it to gain advantage for whatever reason, but it's silly. Now, dialect is something else. Dialect reflects regional speech patterns." I wanted to tape Anna's lilting voice and play it at bedtime every night of my life.

"Dialect also defines social class. There's more to all this, of course.

If you know what to listen for, you can tell where he or she is from, as finite as the name of the village. Also. you can learn their approximate level of affluence.

What you're hearing, or better yet, what Grace is speaking, is plain old gibberish. She's just yanking your chain, Mart."

Anna Mae promised to have dinner with me, "soon". And Anna Mae Wong never breaks a promise.

I wanted to review Wayne's Directory of Classes, specifically the Sciences. I may want to change my major.

\* \* \* \* \* \* \* \*

Grace Yu was a Chinese woman of indeterminate age but determinate wealth. I started figuring her net worth after she led me into her 2-story white stone mansion located next store. I was there to sign the lease.

All four walls were replete with a wide marble mantle that held large assortments of Chinese statues- animals, people, houses, and intricate bamboo-like teahouses with sprawling jade lawns. All were made of jade China. I picked up a small flowerpot. Its flowing lines and exquisite luster shouted gorgeous. I almost dropped it when she yelled.

"Put that down!" Her graceful demeanor had vanished like a hockey puck slapped into the net. "Don't touch them!" Wow. I put my hands in my pockets.

She walked over to a highly polished secretary, sat down, and then spoke which sounded more like a sweetened grunt. "You want?" Rather abrupt, I thought. It might have been the shortest sales pitch in history. I agreed to the terms of the lease and wrote a check for one thousand dollars, the monthly rent.

She accepted it with her right hand, and beckoned to me with her left. "More!" I thought the monthly rent had been agreed to earlier. I couldn't imagine getting a rate increase simply by picking up one of her statues. "More money!" Oh, I got it. More money. She wanted more money probably for the deposit. . "Two thousand!" she said. "Deposit."

After I handed her the additional one thousand dollar check she started spouting out what they call in the Navy, the rules of the road. She was dictating the rules of Brown Street. No this, no that, can't this, can't that! Never this, always that!

A gentleman clad in work clothes and floppy sandals came into the living room. It turned out to be her husband. He didn't look at me. He hardly looked at her. He grunted, too. Something in broken Chinese. She weighed the consequences of what he asked of her. She needed a moment before answering. Finally, she gave him permission, handed him a twenty-dollar bill, and I tnought she unlocked his chain.

"Who was that man, Grace?" I asked.

"Yu?"

"No, who?"

"Me Yu."

"I know that, Grace.Who man?"

"Man husband. "

"Does he work for you?"

"Work for GM."."

"Oh." I wondered if he might be in GM's advertising department. If so, he and I could split an egg roll and thereby have this caper qualify as an expense account item. Stranger numbers have met the criteria.

"He GM research head". Husband looked like a guy about to take trash to curbside and then finish swabbing toilets.

I asked Grace for the key to my condo and left before she could remind me that ceilings were also a perk.

*　*　*　*　*　*　*　*

The condo was just fine. But, it came with an added perk. Her name was Grace, as in Yu, of which there could only be one.

"Grace! I didn't hear you come in. Did you forget something?

"No."

I couldn't imagine what she wanted. "Can I get you anything, Grace, a glass of water perhaps?"

"No."

If Grace was almost anyone else, perhaps if she were a "10"and said, "I'd love to have a drink with you," and brought a come-hither smile to the room, I'd have shred my plans for the evening and joined hr. If Grace was a "10", I'd prolong her visit by asking her if she'd like to stay for dinner.

"All I have are some leftovers. I hope you don't mind." A "10" would say, "Oh anything will do, Mart. I'm not hungry." Be careful when you hear this one. It's right out of the best-seller,Top 100 Common Expressions That Women Never Mean,"(Unless they're married). They're common lines used as filler to keep the conversation moving, but may as well be spoken into to an empty shopping bag. I suggest you not even listen. She doesn't mean a word of it.

If Grace was a "10"- and hell will freeze over before that ever happens - I'd turn on the stereo, lower the lights, and invite her to join me on the couch.

If a "10" says, "I can't stay very long, " ignore it. Act as though she Didn't say anything. She does not mean one word. That line is right out of the Top 100 book.

When you suggest she stay over, and her reply is, "I'd love to but I have an early start in the morning," ignore every word. Walk into your bedroom and turn down the comforter. Chances are, she'll be right behind you. If she's a "10".

For a while I felt my ratings, set from "10" to "0", were too stringent. I found that some women try to qualify, but fall short, even with good intentions. There aren't many "10"'s" waiting to meet us. And why should they? I've been told women have their own tool box -- tape measures, yardsticks, and magnifying glasses --

Have you looked in the mirror lately? Look twice at the clothes you wear? Sharpened your sense of humor? You're mot really funny, but you knew that. Have you faced up to dour shortcomings? Remember what Woody Allen said? "Ninety percent of life is showing up. Think of the last time you just showed up, and no one knew you were standing there – for a half hour – until they left for coffee – without you. see a "10"shopping in the super market, saddled with kids or waiting alone in the rain for a bus."10's" are hard to come by. You're probably looking in the wrong places. Bo to go to the movies alone and d look for a "10" sitting alone. A rare occurrence, but worth arty. Bars are very chancey. Some guys go broke paying for their drinks. They usually go home alone with the early edition of the Free Press.

I decided to lower the acceptance rate to "7". The ensuing weeks Were vapid. Had the "'7s" not heard of my special? I was dismayed.

Grace kept popping in and out like a rabbit. Even when I left for the office. She offered a bank of lame excuses. "I want to take a peek. Maybe time wrong" "Did you use oven yet? Let me know how you like. Don't touch the a/c or heat. Call me. Where do you keep your garbage? Don't leave water running."

One morning when she arrived, I kept holding my breath for as long as I could.

"You sick?"

"No, I'm holding my breath. Because it's the only thing you have showed me to how to do. "Did the toilet run all night?" "Wow.

I thought I'd go nuts with lame excuses. Grace. She was still in my condo, now going through my sox and ties. was still sitting there, providing no inspiration. The Graces of our world aren't born with any number at all. Not even a "0".

Later in the evening, I gave serious thought to dropping it to a "4.5".

Fortunately, ladies with Grace's personality were never approached by guys on the make. Grace could walk naked through the Fox and Hounds, from the front entrance to the far rear tables, amd not have a worry. She could stop for a drink at the bar, and still, no approaches. My problem is that I imagined her husband was the kind of Asian prolific in that Oriental, "Dance of the Knives. I imagined he practiced throwing bread knives at a cardboard dummy, for a reason.

Grace told me she wanted to see if I cleaned the table and the kitchen counter after dinner. No "10" would ever do that.

"Grace, I haven't even eaten yet. Whether I did or did not is none of your business!" She ignored me. So I led her to the kitchen door and out into the rain. I told her she must knock from now on and never, ever enter if I am not here. And maybe when I am here!

I heated some leftovers, and turned on the tv. A new tv show called, "Use Your Imagination" was on. Sounded silly. I switched to CNN.

Grace told me she wanted to see if I cleaned the table and the kitchen counter after dinner. No "10" would ever do that.

"Grace, I haven't even eaten yet. Whether I did or did not is none of your business!" She ignored me. I led her to the kitchen door and out into the rain. I told her she must knock from now on and never, ever enter if I am not here. And maybe when I am here!

I heated some leftovers, and turned on the tv. A new tv show called, "Use Your Imagination" was starting. Sounded silly. I switched to CNN.

The condo was decent in spite of Grace. Visitors arrived in dribs and drabs. Word leaked, like an obituary notice. If you don't think people read those teeney announcements check out the response next time a mutual friend dies. You intend to mention it but everyone already knows.

The guys liked my condo but what do they know? Five of them were rummaging through the refrigerator looking for beer. I felt like Jerry Seinfeld putting up with five Kramers.

I did respect their opinion. Almost all of them were born in Detroit, they live in Birmingham, and know every brick and turn in the neighborhood. The guys left empty-handed. With no beer, there's no reason to stay,

Mary Anne MacGinley, a daughter of a buddy of mine, stopped by unexpectedly the following Saturday afternoon. I was pleased to see her. I hoped no one else would come crashing through while she was there. She thought my condo was "neat". She used one of those words that young people resurrect without realizing it. They think the rest us are hearing their word for the first time. Mary Anne does the same thing with the word "cool." She uses it like she invented it. Few people have an idea of where this word came from. I told her and she listened.That's one of the reasons I liked her.

I remember one night Dizzy was on break after finishing his first set at the Onyx Club on Fifty-Second Street.[1][1] We were discussing the advent of the new jazz sound called bee-bop, which I despised. It was devoid of melody. They also called it by its formal title -- progressive jazz.

Dizzy preached the bible of bee-bop around the world. He had his musicians turn to Psalm Flatted Fifth, before they blew a note.

I asked him why he preferred bee-bop to traditional music. Since the bop I heard sounded like the most complex collection of musical trash I ever heard, I expected an extended explanation. I was wrong.

"I prefer it because it's cool, man."

*  *  *  *  *  *  *  *

MaryAnne knocked me out whenever she used that word. But she could knock me out just by showing up. She sounded like no one else when she spoke. Her froggy voice turned me on. If Mary Anne were to decide to recite the Preamble to the Constitution, everyone else might leave the room but I'd hang out and listen to every word. I once asked her if she was born with the voice she had.

"It probably comes from my smoking."

"I didn't know you smoked!"

"I did. When I was ten. Once."

I wanted to tape her voice and take it to bed with me on cold, lonely nights. She had blue eyes that made everyone else's blue eyes look milky. She had no idea she talked or looked the way she did. Raised with five brothers, Mary Anne was the youngest. The neighbors once asked her mother if it was true that her brothers were training her for the Golden Gloves.

"Are you all nuts? My darling little baby fighting with grown men?

Now where did you hear all this?

That winter MaryAnne tried out for the boys' high school hockey

Team and made kit. She got her letter in senior year.

Mary Anne had been checking out the condo, inside, outside, all around -- and was ready with her opinion.

"I love it! Now, you can practically do whatever you want, and hardly leave your condo! Buy your beer and rent your flicks across the street. The Midtown Cafe is right around the corner and you told me once you like it. You can walk to the Birmingham Theater. You won't need your car for any of that!

"Now who could ask for anything more? And with all of this --- you get me!"

If I had even thought of making a run on this darling little hockey player, I wouldn't even need track shoes.

However, I had other issues. First and foremost, I was married. She was almost too young. Nope. A perfect plan for destruction. So we had coffee on rare occasion. The only time we veered from that small social was when we split a brownie.

Mary Anne was counting on her fingers all of my blessings – beer, a babe, first-run flicks.......She interrupted herself and threw a firecracker into the mix..

"And you're no longer married! Marriage is so yesterday. You've got it made in the shade, babe!"

She gave me a big hug.

"And you've got me!"

Someone must have taken the wrappings off what I thought divorce was all about.

Whenever I stopped at Reid's house, Mary Ann always joined us "to talk business. She toook delight in knowing something I didn't know.

"Guess who the new advertising manager of Chrysler is going to be?" she'd ask. Or, "Guess which agency is gong to lose their largest account?" If I failed to know the answers she'd say, ""Better start making some sales calls, Mr. Toohey!", and we'd all brteak up

# No Help Wanted, Thank You

## Tales of Three Disasters
## Biggie Al T.

Salesmen in branch offices should display this No Help Wanted sign in the hope that their visiting sales managers get the message.

Here's how the dreaded unsolicited help comes about. Mr. biggie in the main office gets a bothersome bug in his anal canal and says to his secretary, "Ruth, call our Detroit guy and tell him I'm coming out!"

Ruth orders a seat on a direct flight and a room at the same hotel as last time.

"Tell him I'll be out next week for four days. I want daily sales calls plus dinners with top level Big 3 guys. No second-hand junior decision makers please." One could almost hear drums rolling as Biggie's pronouncements trickled throughout the building.

"Send a copy of my itinerary to the company brass, our entire sales staff, and our branch guy. Let 'em all know I'm working."

What you have just witnessed is the equivalent of a one--man army about to invade a country without a gun.

"I think Marty needs a little help with those automotive types," says Biggie to his secretary. As a result the branch salesman's own business schedule for that week gets trashed, key names are replaced with showboats so Biggie can rub elbows.

Biggie Al T.'s deportment in client Joe O'Donnell's office is classic. O'Donnell is Ford's top marketing star. New York managers know nothing about cars. They confuse Thunderbird with Firebird, Ghia with Kia, and Alpha Romeo with an Italian restaurant.

Out of the blue, Biggie Al T. asks," Why don't you advertise Ford LTD in our magazine?" Silence. Deafening silence. Joe finally responds. "The average age of the buyers of LTD's is getting close to 60, older than your readers, Al," says Joe. "Much older."

"Does that really matter, Joe? (Oh my god!) Our readers have parents, aunts and uncles who are old enough, don't you see? It's an opportunity to broaden your market." Joe didn't see.

"Al, Ford already places considerable advertising with you on our smaller, more youthful and sporty cars matching the younger demographics of your readers."

It seemed time for Biggie Al T. to shut ut his mouth, thank Joe for the business and change the subject.

"I think you're missing another golden opportunity," persists Biggie Al T. "You've got to compete with the imports. They are still beating your sales figures. The imports are eating Ford's lunch, Joe."

Al T. managed to hit a triple that day. He made an idiotic suggestion that would never fly; he didn't thank Joe for the business; and he insulted Joe with a supposedly clever remark before leaving.

\* \* \* \* \* \* \* \*

As a reader, I think you recognize how senseless Al's proposal was. Later in the week Marty was on the golf course with Joe. "Who was the doofus you brought in last week, Mart." Joe was laughing. "God, he was dense. You guys have to put up with a load. We see it all the time."

Meanwhile, Biggie Al T. is reporting to his big boss in NYC. "I think I pushed Ford toward targeting the imports. I'm glad I gave Marty some muscle by spending a few days with him in Detroit." Al stood still to be congratulated by his boss. "I told Ford to get busy before the imports eat their lunch!" They both laughed. The big boss walked Al back to the elevator. "I guess Detroit still doesn't get the message. But what the hell, Al. At least you tried."

A cynic once said, "When a biggie makes sales calls with you it's as if he's peeing in his blue serge suit. It gives him a warm feeling, but no one really notices."

# BIGGIE DON R.

Re-wind to previous' No Help Wanted caption (above) where Biggie Al 's deportment is a New York classic. They enter the client's office and (continue reading from there).

Biggie Don R., a VP this time, arrives in Detroit. Marty picks him up mad they're off to Kenyon &Eckhardt Advertising. K&E manages the Lincoln-Mercury account. Biggie Don R. suggests Marty set up the presentation boards and the Kodak Carousel gets plugged in.

"Lemmee know when you're ready, Mart. I have two new slides to be added to the Carousel," says Biggie Don R.

"New slides?"asks Marty.

"They fit in where you talk about today's professional-managerial women in the workplace competing with the men. We'll use this slide of Marilyn Monroe."

"Fine." (Marty wished Biggie Don R. had used a latter day business personality instead of a female sex symbol).

"Here's the slide." I noted the slide's cardboard frame was too thick to fit in the Carousel. It was the wrong kind of slide. Don panicked, sees this as a disaster and starts to force the slide in. Marty suggests they forget it and replace it at a later date. Biggie Don R. persists and leans heavily on the slide while cursing under his breath. .

"I got it halfway in but her boobs are too big to fit."

"Don, it's not her boobs. It's the cardboard frame. It's too thick."

Now some of those who intended to view the presentation leave their seats and offer their help. I tell Don, "We are losing our audience." Bruce Andrews, a heavyset K&E senior executive jams the slide in so hard we almost can't get it out.

"Here's the second slide, Mart. This should fit."

"Who is it, Tarzan?" I was being facetious.

"It's Jack Nicklaus."

The slide wouldn't fit. Don says something about Jack's putter not fitting.

"Don, first it's Marilyn's boobs. Then it's Jack's putter. It's the cardboard frame!"

The presentation went very well in spite of boobs and putters.

As for business, I don't think Biggie Don R. would know a Mercury car if he got hit by one. Otherwise he could have made a transition while I was speaking, linking the Mercury Capri to the demographics of our magazine's readers; one of the reasons we were there. Normally, he does this. It helps and gives him a chance to open his mouth instead of standing there like a dressmaker's dummy.

Later, I took Biggie Don R. to lunch. My favorite hangout was always a treat. Don was totally dejected because of his slides. It would have been better if we had lunch alone on the roof.

The afternoon was a wipeout. There were two cancellations. Good, I thought. He'd be useless anyway. We had dinner was at a loud sports bar. It was a play-off game. We couldn't hear a word. I drove back to Don R's hotel. He brought up the slides again.

I had trouble keeping my mouth shut. I wanted to tell him, "Don, enough already.

Give it up! I'm sick of listening to your complaints."

I decided to paraphrase Clark Gable in "Gone With The Wind". "Frankly Donald, I don't give a rat's ass about your can't-live-without slides. I've gotten by fine all this time without them and I could spend the rest of my life with two glaring omissions in the slide tray. Tell Marilyn and Jack I don't have room for them. And that's the truth.

# BIGGIE JOE B.

Re-wind to previous No Help Wanted where Biggie Don and Marty enter K&E's office-- and then continue from there. No need to repeat Biggie's plans to visit Detroit. They're all alike.

Jack Martin, media supervisor, Campbell-Ewald Agency has a word with Marty and Biggie Joe B. C-E manages the Chevrolet account. Martin asks if the presentation can start as soon as possible. He had another meeting following this one. Approximately thirteen media people filled the room- - a nice turnout.

Biggie Joe B. has just been named publisher of C/D and he's dying to tell everyone. Marty is about to start the presentation whenBiggie Joe B. interrupts. "Marty, let me say a few words." I feel it's okay. Only take a minute. He wants the audience to know he's been promoted.

Ten or twelve minutes later, Biggie Joe B. is telling more stories about life in the big city, Jack Martin is looking at me with daggers; Joe continues to lay it on. One person in the audience gets up and leaves – then another.

While Biggie Joe B. is rambling, Marty interrupts Biggie Joe B., who is now circling the room in a pontificating manner.

"Say goodnight, Gracie," says Marty rather loudly. There's a hush in the room followed by a few snickers. Biggie Joe B. feels broadsided. Shocked. He clearly doesn't understand. Marty points to his watch and says, "These people are on the dime, Joe." Marty swings into the board presentation.

Joe still doesn't understand. Marty runs through the pitch in surprising time, covering all sales points and turns in an acceptable job.

Jack Martin walks up to thank Marty with a few words of criticism for Biggie Joe B. who is still pale. He wants to know what Martin said.

Marty and Biggie Joe B. pack up, leave and walk to the coffee stand on the main floor. Over a cup of coffee Biggie Joe B. chastises Marty. " I can understand your concern about time, but the very first thing we learn in Salesmanship 101 is that once you get the attention of the person or people you're trying to sell hold onto them for as long as possible. It is the salesman's time to enjoy his place in the sun."

"Place in the sun? You talked so long I thought you'd get sunburned! They told us to be quick to get 'em back to their office!"

"They always say that Mart. If you listen to that you'd never complete a sales call."

"Well we almost didn't finish this one, Joe.

We drove across town to Darcy Advertising. At the conclusion of, my presentation Joe asked if he could say a few words. I gave him five minutes. Had I not stopped him, he'd still be there, talking to an empty room.